The Law Of Release: Moving From Resistance To Receptivity

VINCENT WB

Published by VINCENT WB, 2025.

First Edition: February 2025

Cover Design: Vincent WB

Editor: Vincent WB

Printed in Kenya – January 2025

For inquiries, permissions, or to share how this book touched your heart, contact:

⬦ **Email:** vincentwbauthor@gmail.com

Published by: Vincent WB

Website: https://vineread.com[1]

Follow the journey:

⬦ Facebook: *Vincent Barasa*

⬦ Instagram: *@vincentwb_author*

---

1. https://vineread.com/

Meet the Author: Vincent WB

Vincent WB is a storyteller of the soul—an author, artist, and creator who believes the deepest truths are found not in noise, but in silence. Born and rooted in Kenya, Vincent writes with the intention to awaken something already living inside you: peace, presence, and the quiet courage to let go.

He writes not to teach, but to remember—with you.

To remind you of what was never truly lost.

His words are mirrors. His pages, invitations.

When not writing, Vincent is often wandering barefoot through nature, journaling by candlelight, or designing book covers that feel like portals. *The Law of Release* is his most personal offering to date—a love letter to surrender, and a companion for anyone learning to breathe again.

This book began as a whisper.

Now, it's in your hands.

Welcome home.

Dedication

To the one who is tired of pretending to be strong.
To the quiet one who's always been the safe place for others, but rarely
for themselves.
To the soul who longs not for more—but for *enoughness*.
This is for you.
May these pages be the breath you didn't know you were holding.
May they remind you:
You are not broken. You are blooming.
With all my heart,
– Vincent WB

Acknowledgement

This book is the result of many silences, countless walks alone, and prayers whispered into the wind. But it is also the fruit of the people who saw me when I forgot myself.

To the ones who held me when I was unraveling—you know who you are. Your presence taught me that healing isn't something we earn. It's something we allow.

To the quiet mornings, the heartbreaks that softened me, the still waters that reflected my becoming—thank you. You were all part of this story.

To every reader holding this book now:
Thank you for your courage to open it.
Thank you for your presence here.
You're not alone anymore.
And above all,
To the Divine whisper that never stopped calling me home—thank You for trusting me to be a mirror.
With reverence,
– Vincent WB

Preface

I didn't write this book from a mountain.
I wrote it from a valley.
It was never meant to be a guidebook. It's a conversation. A
remembering. A letting go.
The Law of Release was born from a place of exhaustion—the kind that
doesn't just drain your energy, but your will to pretend. I didn't want
to be strong anymore. I wanted to be *real*.
And somewhere in that honesty... I found peace.
This isn't a "how-to." It's a "here's what helped."
It's not for the mind to master. It's for the heart to feel.
You don't have to take notes. Just take a breath.
That's where it begins.
– Vincent WB

THE LAW OF RELEASE EXPLAINED

The **Law of Release** is a spiritual and psychological principle that emphasizes the importance of letting go of attachments, fears, limiting beliefs, and emotional baggage in order to experience true freedom, peace, and growth. At its core, this law teaches that in order to move forward in life and embrace new opportunities, you must release what no longer serves you. This includes not only physical possessions or past experiences but also mental, emotional, and spiritual burdens that keep you stuck in old patterns.

When we hold on to negative emotions, unhelpful thoughts, and past hurts, we are essentially resisting the natural flow of life. The Law of Release encourages us to trust in the process of life, accept the present moment, and let go of the need to control outcomes, thus creating space for new possibilities.

How to Apply the Law of Release:

Acknowledge What Needs to Be Released: The first step in applying the Law of Release is becoming aware of what is holding you back. This might include toxic relationships, outdated beliefs, fear of failure, or unhealed emotional wounds. It requires introspection and honesty with yourself. Start by identifying these attachments or burdens, no matter how small they may seem.

Let Go of the Past: Release any attachment to past experiences, mistakes, or regrets. Understand that they are a part of your journey but no longer need to define your future. Forgiveness plays a major role in this process, whether it's forgiving others or forgiving yourself. Holding on to past pain keeps you anchored in old energy, preventing you from stepping into a more empowered future.

Release Control: The Law of Release teaches us to stop trying to control every outcome. Trust that the universe (or life) will unfold as it should. Often, we get caught in the need to control situations, people, or results, which leads to stress and frustration. Letting go of this desire for control opens the door to acceptance and peace.

Cultivate Mindfulness: Practicing mindfulness helps you to stay present and observe your thoughts and emotions without judgment. This awareness allows you to recognize when you're clinging to old stories or patterns. By being present, you can more easily release unnecessary attachments and embrace the present moment.

Embrace Impermanence: Life is constantly changing. Embracing the impermanence of everything around you allows you to release your attachment to things, people, or situations that are transient. By acknowledging that change is inevitable, you learn to flow with life rather than resist it.

Practice Self-Compassion: The Law of Release is not about forcing yourself to let go, but rather about being gentle and compassionate with yourself as you do. Be patient with the process. Letting go can be painful, but practicing self-compassion will help you heal and move forward with grace.

Release Expectations: The Law of Release also applies to our expectations. We often hold on to certain outcomes or timelines, but life doesn't always unfold the way we expect. By releasing rigid expectations and embracing life as it is, we cultivate a sense of peace and ease. Trust that the path you are on will unfold in the perfect way for you, even if it's not exactly as you imagined.

Practice Gratitude: Gratitude helps shift your focus from what you lack or need to release to what you already have. It is a grounding practice that reminds you of the abundance in your life. When you release what no longer serves you, you make room for new blessings and opportunities to enter. Gratitude opens the door to new possibilities and helps you stay centered in the present moment.

Letting Go of Negative Self-Talk: One of the most significant areas to apply the Law of Release is in how you speak to yourself. Negative self-talk, self-criticism, and limiting beliefs often keep you stuck in a cycle of fear and doubt. To release these, you need to practice positive affirmations, self-acceptance, and the understanding that you are enough as you are.

Introduction

There is a moment—quiet, almost invisible—when something shifts inside us. Not because we learned something new... but because we finally *remembered* something ancient.

That moment is what this book is about.

The Law of Release isn't a technique. It's not a trend. It's a way of being that unravels resistance and lets life flow again. It's the gentle art of no longer fighting what wants to be felt, seen, healed, or held.

At its heart, this book is a story—about Noah, a man much like you and me. Searching. Grieving. Hiding behind a smile. Until life gently brought him back to what he had forgotten:

That peace isn't something we find.

It's something we stop resisting.

This is not the end of your search.

This is the beginning of your surrender.

Welcome to *The Law of Release*.

Let's begin...

— Vincent WB

Prologue

The Weight We Don't Know We're Carrying
Before the breath, there was the noise.
Before the letting go, there was the grip.
And before Noah remembered who he was, he forgot a thousand times.
This is not a story of becoming someone new.
It's a story of returning to what was always there.
When we are young, we learn to hold on—
to ideas, to expectations, to the ache of proving we are enough.
We armor up. We strive. We survive.
But somewhere along the way, the soul grows quiet beneath all the doing.
And one day, if we're lucky—or cracked open by life—we stop.
And we listen.
Noah didn't go looking for a transformation.
He was simply tired.
Tired of fixing. Tired of forcing. Tired of pretending healing was a checklist.
What he found instead was a law not written in books or spoken in loud rooms.
It was written in silence.
Etched in the wind, the breath, the stillness between words.
It whispered:
You don't have to carry what isn't yours.
You don't have to become anything other than who you already are.

Release.
And remember.
This is that story.
Of one man.
Of all of us.
Of the quiet return to self.
Not through doing. But through allowing.
Not through answers. But through presence.
Not by force. But by grace.
Welcome to *The Law of Release.*
May it meet you not where you are striving—
but where you are soft enough to receive.

THE LAW OF RELEASE: MOVING FROM RESISTANCE TO RECEPTIVITY

PART 1: THE BREAKING POINT

The sound of morning rain tapping gently on the windowpane was the first thing Noah Ellison noticed. It was the soft, rhythmic kind—almost musical—the sort of rain that made the city glisten like polished steel. He lay in bed for a few moments, eyes half open, his breathing slow and even, feeling the weight of the duvet draped over him like a second skin. The ambient hum of the city, muffled by glass and concrete, stirred something inside him that he couldn't quite name.

His alarm had gone off twenty minutes earlier, a melodic tone set to ease him awake rather than jolt him. Noah rarely needed it. His body clock was a machine: precise, consistent, obedient. Every weekday morning, he rose at 6:00 a.m., and by 6:30, he was dressed in his soft charcoal hoodie and running shoes, Apple Watch synced, steps logged.

But today, he lingered.

There was no reason, really. His schedule was tight, his calendar booked. Stand-ups. Sprint reviews. A pitch meeting with the design team at 2:00 p.m. And yet something in his chest held him still—as if his body, like the sky, sensed a shift on the horizon.

Claire stirred beside him, murmured something in her sleep, and turned toward the wall. Her dark hair fanned across the pillow like ink spilled on snow. For a moment, Noah watched her, his gaze softening.

They'd been together three years—long enough to settle into a rhythm, short enough to still be guessing at each other's silences.

With a quiet exhale, he slipped out of bed.

Noah's apartment in the South of Market neighborhood was sleek and modern, all clean lines and soft lighting. A minimalist's dream. Floor-to-ceiling windows wrapped around the corner of the unit, offering a misty view of the San Francisco skyline. On clear days, you could see all the way to the Bay Bridge, a sight that had once filled him with quiet pride.

He moved through the kitchen like a man in rehearsal: pour the beans, set the grind, start the water. The Chemex rested on the counter like an altar to his daily ritual. He took his coffee black—no sugar, no milk. Purity in process. Control in small things.

By 7:15, he was on his usual jogging route, the soles of his shoes whispering against wet pavement. He ran past storefronts still shuttered in early morning light, the quiet whirr of the city beginning to rise like a sleeping giant. At the Embarcadero, he paused to stretch, inhaling deeply, letting the air fill his lungs and the ocean wind brush against his skin.

His mind was already ahead of him—thinking through deliverables, planning how to push back on unrealistic timelines, wondering if Claire would bring up the topic again tonight. Marriage. Babies. The next step.

Noah was thirty-five, a senior product manager at a fast-scaling AI company that promised to "Revolutionize the Way Humans and Technology Co-Create." It was the kind of place with kombucha on tap, nap pods, and leadership books scattered like confetti across breakout rooms. He was good at his job. Exceptionally so. Strategic. Analytical. Articulate. He could turn chaos into clarity with a single slide deck. His team respected him. His boss trusted him. Investors liked his pitch.

But lately, there was a buzz beneath the surface—a friction he couldn't name. He noticed it in the way his jaw tensed during meetings, in the heaviness that clung to him during otherwise quiet moments. He was always "on," always efficient, always producing. And yet... somewhere in that flow, something essential had gone missing.

By 8:30, Noah stood before the full-length mirror in the bedroom, adjusting the cuffs of his slate-blue button-down. His jaw was clean-shaven. His eyes were sharp, if a bit tired. From the outside, he looked like someone who had it all figured out.

"Big day?" Claire asked from the bathroom, brushing her hair.

Noah nodded, tying his watch around his wrist. "Just the usual circus."

Claire leaned in the doorway, watching him. "You've been quiet lately."

He offered a small smile, one that didn't quite reach his eyes. "Just focused."

She stepped closer, reaching out to straighten his collar. "I miss the days you weren't always so focused."

There it was again—that gentle nudge toward something softer, slower. A different pace of life. He kissed her forehead and left the words unsaid.

At work, everything moved like a current he could no longer resist. Notifications blinked. Meetings blurred. Ideas buzzed. He stood at the center of it all like a conductor guiding an orchestra on the edge of crescendo. But beneath the noise, something in him was unraveling.

Around noon, during a product review, one of the engineers brought up a potential flaw in the upcoming launch. It wasn't catastrophic, but it was enough to warrant pause.

Noah's voice was calm, measured. "We'll assess risk after the demo, but for now, let's keep momentum."

The engineer frowned. "That's not really addressing the—"

"I said we'll assess it after the demo." The sharpness in his tone surprised even him.

The room went still for a beat.

Someone coughed. Laptops clicked. The meeting continued.

That evening, Noah sat alone in his car just outside his apartment building. The rain had started again—heavier now, drumming against the windshield. His hands rested on the steering wheel, motionless. He should have been upstairs by now. Claire had texted him to pick up Thai. He had, and the smell of lemongrass and chili filled the cabin.

But he couldn't move. Couldn't will himself to step into the rhythm he had so carefully constructed. The silence inside the car felt louder than anything he'd heard all day.

He thought of his father then—a man who had lived his entire life with quiet precision, a man who had never once cried in front of him. A man who died of a heart attack at fifty-three, still clinging to unspoken dreams.

Noah was thirty-five. The age his father had started saying, "Someday."

What if he was already living someone else's version of success?

The thought struck like a match.

Later that night, after a quiet dinner and lukewarm conversation, Noah stood alone on the apartment balcony. The city below shimmered with a thousand stories, each one moving, aching, dreaming. Claire had gone to bed early. She didn't ask about his mood. Maybe she'd stopped needing to know.

The rain had eased, leaving the scent of ozone and wet concrete hanging in the air. He looked up at the stars, barely visible through the city glow.

And for the first time in a long while, he let himself ask a dangerous question:

What if control was the very thing holding me back?

The answer didn't come. Not yet.

But something inside him had shifted. A quiet rupture in the wall he'd built around himself. The beginning of something unnamed. Something raw.

The calm before the real storm.

And somewhere deep within him, a story had just begun to write itself.

The catalyst – a sudden collapse

It started with a calendar invite.

Noah almost didn't notice it—wedged between back-to-back meetings and a barrage of Slack notifications. The subject line read, "Quick Sync – 11:30 AM – Mandatory." No agenda. No context. Just the cold, clipped efficiency of a corporate summons. The kind that sent a ripple through your gut before your brain even caught up.

He walked into the boardroom with his usual composure, shoulders squared, expression unreadable. The room was already full—his manager, Kara; the Director of HR, a woman named Lillian he barely spoke to; and above all, Jonathan Vance, the company's Chief Operating Officer, who rarely attended anything short of an emergency.

Noah's pulse ticked up.

"Hey," he said, trying to smile as he settled into the only open seat at the table. "Didn't realize this was a party."

No one laughed.

Jonathan leaned forward, fingers steepled. "Noah, thanks for joining us. Let's get straight to it."

The air shifted. Just like that.

Kara kept her eyes on the table. Lillian opened a folder.

Jonathan spoke with the cool precision of someone who had done this many times. "After careful evaluation, we've decided to make some organizational changes—realignment for long-term strategic goals. Unfortunately, that means your role is being dissolved, effective immediately."

Noah blinked. "Wait—what?"

Jonathan didn't flinch. "This isn't a reflection of your performance. The company is evolving, and—"

"You're firing me," Noah said, louder than he intended.

A beat of silence.

Kara finally looked up, her voice hushed. "We're offering you a very generous severance package. And of course, we'll support you through this transition."

Transition. Like he was crossing the street.

Noah laughed under his breath, incredulous. "You're firing me in the middle of a sprint. I'm managing three core products. I onboarded two new PMs last quarter. And no one had the decency to give me a heads-up?"

"We wanted to avoid unnecessary disruption," Lillian offered gently.

"Oh, I see," he snapped. "You wanted to avoid *your* disruption. Mine's just collateral damage."

"Noah—" Kara started, but he stood, heart pounding.

"This is bullsh—"

"Please don't make this harder than it needs to be."

Jonathan's voice was final. A gavel falling.

Noah's mouth opened, then closed. There were too many things to say, none of them safe. He was suddenly hyperaware of everything: the soft whirr of the AC, the dull ache in his temple, the way Lillian quietly pushed a manila envelope across the table toward him like a condolence card.

He took it. Walked out.

The elevator ride down was silent except for the buzz in his ears. Noah stared at his reflection in the brushed metal doors, seeing a version of himself he no longer recognized. Dismissed. Discarded. A liability in a tailored shirt.

By the time he stepped outside, the sun had broken through the clouds, casting an ironic golden hue across Market Street. People passed by, oblivious. The world spun on, unbothered by the implosion of a life.

He walked for blocks without direction, weaving through crowds, past cafés and buskers and delivery vans. At some point, he realized he was holding the severance envelope like a lifeline, fingers crumpling the corners. He stuffed it into his bag.

His phone buzzed. A text from Claire.

Can we talk when you get home?

Five words. That was it. No emojis. No heart. Just the digital equivalent of a whisper in the dark.

When he pushed through the apartment door, the air inside felt too still. Claire was curled up on the couch, legs tucked beneath her, like she had been waiting there all day.

He dropped his bag by the counter and didn't say anything for a long moment.

She looked up. "Hey."

He took a breath. "I got fired."

Her eyes widened. "Oh my God. What? Why?"

"Corporate 'realignment,'" he said, voice flat. "Just like that. No warning. One minute I'm pitching strategy, the next I'm packing my desk."

Claire stood slowly, approaching him. She placed a hand on his arm. "Noah, I'm so sorry."

He nodded, jaw clenched.

"I—" She stopped herself, like she was swallowing the rest of the sentence.

"What?" he asked, voice brittle. "Just say it."

"I've been... unhappy," she said softly.

He blinked, confused. "Claire—"

"I didn't want to bring it up like this. Not today. But I can't keep pretending everything's fine. I've felt distant for months, and I didn't know how to say it."

Noah stepped back, as if her words had weight. "Distant?"

"I don't know who you are lately, Noah. You're always in your head. Always working. Always performing. I feel like I'm living with a machine that's programmed for success, not a person."

"That's not fair," he said, heat rising in his chest.

"Isn't it?" she whispered.

A long silence stretched between them.

He looked at her—really looked at her. The lines of worry on her face, the tears threatening behind her eyes. This wasn't an ambush. This was a breaking point she'd been holding back for far too long.

"I just need space," she added, voice trembling. "To figure out what I want. Who I am. Who we are—if we even *are* anything anymore."

Noah felt the floor shift beneath him.

"You're leaving," he said, not quite a question.

"I'm not saying forever," Claire replied, eyes glistening. "But I need time. And you... you need to stop holding it all together like your life depends on it. Because something's breaking, Noah. And I think it's you."

That night, the apartment was too quiet.

He sat on the floor beside the couch, phone dark, the manila envelope still unopened beside him. The rain returned, drumming against the windows like it had the morning before. But now it sounded different—harder. Relentless.

He stared out at the city lights, scattered and blinking in the mist. Each one a life. A story. None of them his.

For the first time in years, Noah had nothing to do. Nowhere to be. No version of himself to perform.

Just silence.

And the terrifying freedom of a blank page.

The aftermath – alone with the ruins

The morning arrived without asking for permission.

Noah sat on the edge of his bed, elbows on knees, staring at the half-closed blinds. Thin slats of sunlight broke through, slicing the room into lines of shadow and light—prison bars, almost. The air was too still, like the apartment was holding its breath along with him.

The silence pressed down.

No Slack pings. No calendar alerts. No Claire humming in the kitchen, barefoot and absentmindedly singing the wrong lyrics to old Bon Iver songs.

Just stillness. Heavy and unfamiliar.

The shirt he'd worn yesterday lay crumpled on the floor. His work bag, unzipped and abandoned by the counter, spilled out its contents—an overachiever's time capsule. Laptop charger. Noise-canceling headphones. Three Pilot G2 pens. A small whiteboard marker with someone else's initials on the cap. The manila envelope from HR, still untouched.

He dragged himself to the kitchen.

The Chemex sat where he'd left it the day before—half-washed, stained with the remnants of a ritual that no longer made sense. He reached for his favorite ceramic mug, the one Claire had given him their first Christmas together. Hand-thrown clay, cobalt blue glaze, tiny imperfections he used to trace with his thumb while deep in thought.

It slipped from his fingers.

Shattered on the tile floor.

Noah stared at it for a long time.

Something about the sound—it didn't feel real. Like it had come from a movie he'd seen once, long ago, about a man losing everything in slow motion.

"I'll fix it," he muttered, crouching to gather the pieces. "It's not... that bad."

But it was. The handle had snapped off cleanly. A crack zigzagged through the center like a scar. It was beyond repair.

Still, he tried to fit the shards together with trembling fingers, as if holding it just right would make it whole again.

Just like his job.

Just like Claire.

Just like *himself.*

He sat on the couch in yesterday's jeans, not really seeing anything. The TV was off. His phone, face down. The Spotify app on his laptop had auto-played a melancholic indie playlist he hadn't changed in months. One song looped softly—an ambient track filled with rising violins and voices echoing like ghosts in the mist.

It played.

And played.

And played.

He didn't stop it.

The mind is a cruel thing in stillness. It doesn't offer peace. It replays the worst parts in HD clarity.

The meeting room. Jonathan's unreadable face.

Claire, standing with her arms crossed, holding back tears as she said, "I need space."

The mug, shattered.

The silence.

His jaw clenched. A voice in him—sharp, cold—whispered:

You should've seen this coming.

You should've worked harder.

You let it all slip.

Another voice, louder, angrier:

This wasn't your fault.

Kara should've fought for you.

Claire should've stayed.

Back and forth.

Blame. Denial. Rationalization.

He stood up, paced the apartment like a caged animal.

What now?

What the hell now?

He opened the fridge. Empty but for oat milk, leftover pad thai, and a wilting bunch of kale he'd promised himself he'd cook "someday."

He slammed it shut.

By mid-morning, the apartment felt like a museum of a life that no longer belonged to him.

In the hallway closet, he found an old storage box marked **Noah – College**. He hadn't opened it in years. On a whim, he pulled it out and sat on the floor, legs crossed like a child at story time.

Inside were fragments of another self:

- A photo of him with a robotics team, younger and smiling too wide.
- A letter from his mother, written in careful script: *"We're so proud of you, baby. You've always been the one who holds it all together."*
- A half-finished sketch of a tree, drawn in charcoal—something he'd started during a week of insomnia junior year and never finished.
- A notebook with the words **Prove them wrong** scribbled on the inside cover.

He closed it quickly.

The words burned.

Memory came in sudden, sharp images.

He was ten, sitting at the dining table with a worksheet in front of him. Fractions. Numbers swimming.

"You're smart," his father had said, standing behind him. "No mistakes this time."

Noah had nodded, trying not to let his hand shake as he picked up the pencil.

Later that night, he'd erased the B+ from his test and rewritten it as an A in thick marker before showing it to his parents. Just a small lie. Just enough to keep the illusion intact.

Because anything less than perfect felt like failure.

Now, decades later, the pattern remained. A life built on excellence. Performance. Control.

He had climbed every rung. Won every title. Kept every plate spinning.

And yet, here he was.

Surrounded by silence.

Holding pieces.

He stared at the broken mug again, now resting on the counter in a sad little pile. A symbol of everything he'd tried to glue together in his life—too much weight on the cracks. Not enough care to rest.

Eventually, he found himself back at the window, watching the clouds drift across the San Francisco skyline. The city looked different today. Not threatening. Not dazzling.

Just... indifferent.

He whispered into the quiet:

"I don't know who I am without the work."

And somewhere inside, a deeper truth echoed back:

You never really knew.

His shoulders slumped. The air around him didn't change. The world didn't bend. But something in him softened—just a little.

For the first time, he didn't reach for his to-do list. He didn't check LinkedIn. He didn't pretend.

He just stood there, with no answers.

Only the ruins.

And maybe—if he listened long enough—the start of something honest.

The encounter – a mysterious stranger at the station

It wasn't a conscious decision, walking toward the train station.

Noah hadn't planned to leave the apartment that day. He'd woken up past noon, surrounded by the same silence that had haunted him since everything collapsed. The city outside his window buzzed with weekend energy—bike tires spinning, car horns barking, the occasional laugh from somewhere he couldn't see.

He got dressed in yesterday's clothes. Threw on a jacket. Left without locking the door.

The streets blurred around him. His feet led the way, as if they had their own intelligence, a compass buried in muscle memory. He passed storefronts he didn't recognize, alleyways that narrowed into dreamlike corridors, murals he swore weren't there before.

And then the city quieted.

The sky had softened to a pale gray-blue, and just ahead—tucked between a boarded-up bookstore and a dry cleaner with faded awnings—was a narrow staircase that led down.

A station. One he didn't remember ever seeing.

The sign overhead read: **Crescent Terminal.**

Letters chipped, barely hanging on.

Noah hesitated at the top. He half-laughed. "I don't take trains."

But something pulled at him.

He descended.

The platform was empty. Quiet. Too quiet.

Dust floated in golden shafts of light that broke through high, grimy windows. The far wall was tiled in old blue porcelain, cracked and stained with time. There was no schedule, no noise, no hum of tracks. Just a strange stillness—like the station was asleep and dreaming of better days.

He turned in a slow circle. That's when he saw her.

She was sitting on the far bench, legs crossed, draped in a flowing indigo shawl that caught the light like water. Her hair was a cascade of loose curls, silver and midnight, and her eyes... her eyes stopped him cold.

Not because they were beautiful—though they were. But because they looked at him like they knew.

Not *who* he was.

What he was.

She smiled, just barely. "You're early."

Noah blinked. "Excuse me?"

She tilted her head. "Most people don't show up until the unraveling is complete. You—" she paused, narrowing her gaze, "—still have some edges intact."

He stared at her, unsure if he should walk away or sit down beside her.

"What is this place?" he asked, glancing around.

"A threshold," she replied, as if it were obvious. "Between who you were and who you'll become."

He frowned. "Okay. Cool. Are you... waiting for a train?"

She laughed—a soft, musical sound, like wind through reeds. "No. I'm waiting for you."

He took a cautious step closer, searching for the trick, the punchline, the camera hidden behind a bench.

"I think you've mistaken me for someone else," he said carefully.

"No," she said, eyes steady. "I haven't."

He sat without meaning to. It was like gravity shifted around her. Like she *bent* space in small ways.

She reached into a satchel at her side and pulled out something wrapped in cloth. She unwrapped it slowly and placed it in his hands.

A leather-bound journal.

The cover was worn, dark, and soft as skin. Embossed in fading gold script were the words:

The Law of Release

He opened it. The pages were blank.

"What is this?" he asked.

"An invitation," she said, her voice low. "To let go. To fall without grasping. To remember who you are beneath the armor of ambition."

"I think you're confusing me for someone more... poetic," Noah muttered, flipping through the empty pages.

She studied him for a moment.

"Noah," she said, and he froze.

He hadn't told her his name.

"You've built your life on resistance," she continued. "Control. Order. But something deeper is asking for your attention now. That ache in your chest isn't grief. It's truth knocking."

He felt like the air had thickened. Like he was underwater, breathing but slow. Every word she spoke vibrated somewhere behind his ribs.

"This is insane," he murmured.

"Is it?" she asked, still smiling. "Or is it the first sane thing you've heard in years?"

He looked down at the journal again. It felt warm in his hands. Familiar.

"And if I don't accept it?" he asked.

She shrugged. "Then nothing changes. You rebuild your tower. You polish the ruins. You learn to live with the ache."

He looked at her, something like fear and curiosity coiling in his gut. "And if I do?"

She leaned in. Whispered it like a secret not meant for the air:

"Then you fall. And discover you were never falling at all."

A soft chime echoed through the station. A breeze swept across the platform, scattering old ticket stubs and dust. When he looked back up, she was gone.

Vanished. As if she'd never been there.

He stood slowly, journal clutched to his chest.

No train came.

No announcements.

Just the quiet echo of his own heartbeat and the strange sensation that something had changed. That a door had opened.

He climbed the stairs back to the street, blinking against the sudden light.

Crescent Terminal was gone.

In its place: a dead-end alley with a rusted gate.

But the journal remained in his hands.

And something in him—something soft, cracked open and raw—wanted to write.

Resistance takes root – denial, anger, and avoidance

The journal sat on his kitchen table like it had been placed there by someone else—like it had followed him home.

Noah had tossed it onto the counter last night, then circled it for hours, pretending he didn't care. But every time he left the room, his eyes found it again. Watching. Waiting. Whispering its presence through silence.

By morning, the temptation was too loud.

He poured himself burnt coffee from the half-cleaned Chemex and sat down in front of it like it was an enemy he couldn't ignore. The leather cover still held the faint warmth of memory. Something in him hoped the pages would still be blank. That Mira was just a figment. A trick his brain had played to survive collapse.

But when he flipped it open, the first page now held words.

"Resistance is the mind's last fortress.

It dresses as logic.

It speaks in fear.

It keeps you from your real life while convincing you you're already living it."

– The Law of Release

Noah let out a dry, humorless laugh. "Oh, great. Now the book's judging me too."

He closed it. Hard.

And then, without thinking, opened Instagram.

Thirty-seven minutes passed in an undetected blur—memes, reels, ex-girlfriends' weddings, influencer dogs wearing hats, a guy doing kettlebell squats on a mountain.

He only noticed the time because his phone battery died in his hand.

"Of course," he muttered, tossing it across the couch.

The rest of the day unraveled like a man avoiding gravity.

He vacuumed half of the living room. Reorganized his spice rack alphabetically. Started—then abandoned—a YouTube tutorial on "How to Reset Your Career After Being Blindsided."

At one point, he even Googled Mira's name. Nothing. No profiles. No articles. But when he walked by **Strata Books** on the corner of Mission and 18th, a flyer in the window caught his eye.

Author Night: MIRA DELANEY

"Writing Into the Unknown: Honoring the Inner Collapse"

Friday @ 7PM

His breath caught.

The photo was unmistakable—those silver curls, that same gaze. He stared like the glass might dissolve if he blinked.

But the date was from *three years ago*.

What the hell was going on?

That night, Noah dreamed of water. A wide, still lake under a violet sky. He stood on a crumbling dock, holding the journal, while invisible hands tugged at his sleeves, his thoughts, his chest.

He stepped toward the edge.

A voice whispered—**"Let go."**

But he turned and ran.

When he woke, his sheets were tangled around his legs, drenched in sweat. The journal sat open on his nightstand, even though he was sure he'd left it in the kitchen.

By midweek, resistance had become his roommate.

He began talking to himself out loud. Justifying. Arguing.

"You think I'm afraid of *what*? Being human? I've been through worse."

"You want me to release? Release *what*, exactly? My mortgage? My dignity?"

"What even *is* the real me?"

He put the journal in the freezer. Then the trash. Then, finally, under a stack of old *The Atlantic* magazines—where important things went to be forgotten with class.

He ignored texts from friends. Dodged calls from his mother. When Jake, his best friend, messaged "Drinks? Just wanna check in," Noah responded with a thumbs-up emoji and ghosted him for two days.

He told himself it was space. Recovery. Solitude.

But mostly it was shame.

There was a particular moment—Wednesday night, around 10:30—when the emotional dam almost broke. He sat on the floor, back against the fridge, scrolling aimlessly with a bag of tortilla chips in his lap. A reel came up of a father cradling his newborn, whispering, "You don't have to be anything. You're already enough."

Noah clicked away fast.

But not before he felt the lump in his throat.

Not before he saw, in some strange overlay, his ten-year-old self with graphite-stained hands, frantically erasing a math mistake before his dad could see it.

He walked at night to clear his head.

One evening, he passed a street musician playing something haunting on the violin—slow, aching, beautiful. For a moment, Noah stood completely still.

And then the musician looked up.

Just for a second.

And her eyes—green and flickering with firelight—were **Mira's**.

He stepped forward.

But a group of tourists passed between them. When they cleared, the musician was gone.

Not a trace.

The song still rang in his ears, like it had branded itself to memory.

That night, he retrieved the journal.

His hands shook a little. Maybe from exhaustion. Maybe from something deeper—fear disguised as caffeine withdrawal.

He turned past the first page. The next one was blank, save for a question written in small, delicate script at the top:

"What have you refused to feel?"

He stared at it for a long time.

Didn't write.

Didn't need to—he already knew the answer.

Everything.

All of it.

Grief.

Anger.

Failure.

Loneliness.

Longing.

The terrifying possibility that if he let go of his old life, there might be... nothing.

Or worse—**someone he didn't recognize.**

He closed the journal softly this time. Held it like a fragile heartbeat.

For the first time in days, he whispered the truth out loud:

"I'm not okay."

And the silence that followed felt... different.

Not empty.

Just waiting.

A glimpse of the journey ahead – cracks in the armor
The city had gone to sleep, and so had most of Noah's defiance.
It was 2:13 a.m. His apartment sat in shadow, save for the soft amber of a single floor lamp that bathed the hardwood in quiet gold. The air was still, the kind that holds breath between moments, not yet ready to exhale.

Noah stood at the window, watching the empty street below, one hand resting against the cold glass. He felt hollow—but no longer numb. More like something inside him had shifted slightly out of place, just enough to let the ache in.

Behind him, the journal waited.

It had been sitting on his nightstand for three days now—unmoved, unopened, but never far from thought. Every time he passed it, he felt the quiet pull of something unspoken.

Tonight, he gave in.

He walked over slowly and sat on the edge of his bed, journal in his lap, hands tentative.

He opened it.

The page wasn't blank.

The ink shimmered faintly, like it had only just dried, even though he hadn't touched it.

_"There is a sacred beauty in the breaking.
Because only what breaks can be made new.
And only what is surrendered can be transformed."_

Noah read the words once, twice.

By the third time, his eyes blurred.

He didn't know what part of him cracked first. Maybe it was the memory of his father's tight-lipped silence when he brought home a B. Or maybe it was the way Claire used to curl into him on Sundays, her breath warm against his neck, before that warmth cooled into distance.

Or maybe it was none of that. Maybe it was just the simple truth that he was tired of pretending.

The tears came without warning—silent and hot, carving trails down his cheeks, sliding past his jaw and into the crook of his neck. He didn't sob. He didn't shudder.

He *breathed*.

For the first time in weeks, maybe longer.

Not for control.

Not to hold something back.

But as a release.

It felt like drowning backwards—rising up through pressure and dark, breaking through the surface of something he didn't know had been suffocating him.

He wiped his face with the sleeve of an old hoodie and laughed softly, like the sound surprised him.

The journal still lay open on his lap, its pages holding space for him.

He closed it gently, as if tucking in a child, and walked barefoot to the kitchen drawer.

There, nestled between mismatched batteries and unused birthday candles, was an old tea-light in a brass tin. He took it out, lit it with a trembling hand, and placed it on the windowsill.

The flame flickered once, then held steady—small, warm, alive.

He stood there for a moment, just watching it.

Then he did something strange.

He opened his laptop, clicked through the drafts folder, and hovered over the email he'd been writing to his old boss for days—crafted and re-crafted to defend himself, to explain, to *win* the final word.

He read it one last time.

Then pressed **delete**.

No fanfare. No confirmation box. Just gone.

He shut the laptop and looked back at the flame. It swayed gently, like it approved.

Then, on an instinct he didn't entirely understand, he walked to the front door and—after a moment of hesitation—unlocked it.

Not because he expected someone.

But because something in him had. Finally. Let go.

And just like that, a quiet chapter of his life closed.

The stillness that followed was not empty—but full.

Of questions. Of breath.

Of beginnings.

PART 2: A STRANGER AT THE STATION

Noah wanders – lost in the city and himself

The sky hung low and colorless, like a sheet pulled too tight over a tired world. Even the sun seemed reluctant to show its face.

Noah stepped outside with no plan—only the weight of everything he'd tried not to feel pressing against his chest. He zipped up his jacket against the wind, shoved his hands into his pockets, and started walking.

The city didn't care.

Its streets thrummed with the same chaotic rhythm they always had: buses hissing at red lights, the clatter of impatient heels on concrete, a food truck belting out bachata from tinny speakers. And yet, for Noah, it all felt strangely muted, like he was watching a life he used to belong to from behind a pane of glass.

He didn't answer his phone when it buzzed. Claire had stopped texting after a string of unread messages. Jake had tried once more—"Dude, just let me know you're okay?"—but even that sat unopened. The truth was, Noah didn't know if he was okay. He wasn't sure what that meant anymore.

As he wandered, the city became a blur of half-familiar corners and faded echoes. The bench where he and Claire used to eat falafel after gallery nights. The park where he'd called his mother to tell her about his promotion, voice shaking with pride. A bookstore window where a dusty copy of *The Road Less Traveled* seemed to look back at him with ironic patience.

His legs kept moving, but his mind unraveled in pieces.

He remembered being twelve, building a Lego city in his bedroom with painstaking precision—each building symmetrical, each street perfectly aligned. His father had walked in, smiled tightly, and said, "Looks good. Now take it apart and build something better." Noah hadn't touched Legos again for a year.

He remembered Claire asleep beside him last winter, snow tapping the windows, her hand resting lightly on his chest. He remembered how peaceful she'd looked, how he'd wondered in silence whether love meant feeling safe—or feeling seen.

He remembered the moment last week when the senior VP looked across the conference table and said, "You've lost your edge, Noah." Just like that. In front of everyone.

Now he couldn't remember what edge they were talking about.

Dusk began to fall.

The light dimmed into violet smog, and a chill curled through the city's bones. Noah found himself drifting farther from the places he knew. The streets narrowed, buildings pressed closer together, and graffiti gave way to ivy. The city seemed older here—quieter, like it had fallen out of time.

And then, like it had been waiting for him all along, he saw it.

A train station.

Not the polished chaos of Union Square or the tech-tinged efficiency of Embarcadero. This place was different. Hidden. Half-swallowed by ivy and shadow. It crouched at the end of a narrow lane framed by iron fences and half-bloomed camellia bushes. The kind of place people forgot existed—or assumed had always been closed.

He stepped toward it without thinking, pulled by a silence deeper than the streets he'd left behind.

The faded sign above the arched entry read: **EASTWARD STATION**. The paint had peeled, but the letters still held their shape, like they refused to be erased.

Inside, it was nearly empty.

Old mosaic tiles whispered beneath his shoes as he walked. The ceiling rose into dusky arches, and soft light streamed through a stained-glass window overhead—a sunburst caught in permanent twilight. Dust danced in the glow, slow and sacred.

The ticket booths were unmanned. Benches lined the perimeter like weary sentinels. A clock above the far wall ticked with a rhythm both real and not. Everything smelled of wood, old books, and the kind of rain that never quite falls.

Noah sat on one of the benches.

He didn't know why he felt like he belonged there.

He just did.

His breath misted slightly in the cool air. The silence wasn't oppressive—it felt like a pause between heartbeats. The kind of silence that asks, *Are you ready yet?*

He closed his eyes, and the weight of his body eased.

In the back of his mind, a whisper—half-memory, half-thought—rose to the surface:

"Some stations don't take you where you want to go.

They take you where you're needed."

The line felt familiar. Maybe something from the journal. Or maybe Mira's voice, echoing through some unseen space.

Noah opened his eyes again. A single platform stretched beyond the station's doors, empty and hushed, lit by one flickering lantern. There was no train in sight. No schedule. Just the platform—and a feeling.

That something—or someone—was coming.

He stayed there, unmoving, breath steady.

For the first time in days, he didn't want to escape his thoughts. He wanted to listen.

To what, he wasn't sure yet.

But something in him had started to crack—just enough to let in the quiet.

Just enough to begin again.

The first glimpse – Mira's arrival

The station remained still, hushed like the space between notes in a half-forgotten lullaby.

Noah sat slouched on the weathered bench, elbows on his knees, his gaze fixed somewhere between the mosaic tiles and the past. The platform beyond the arched doorway stretched out in muted grays, lit only by a dim lantern that swung gently in a breeze that shouldn't have existed inside.

He didn't know how long he'd been there.

Time had started to feel more like temperature—something that pressed against his skin rather than ticked in measurable units.

He heard the footsteps before he saw her.

Soft. Measured. Almost musical in their rhythm. Not hurried, not hesitant—just present. Each step landed with the calm assurance of someone who knew exactly where she was, and why she'd come.

Noah sat up instinctively, eyes drawn toward the far end of the station.

There she was.

A woman, maybe mid-thirties—or maybe ageless—walked slowly across the tiled floor. Her dark hair spilled past her shoulders, slightly windswept, as if she'd just stepped off a train from a world with softer weather. She wore a long slate-blue coat, belted at the waist, and brown boots that echoed faintly as she moved. Slung across her shoulder was a satchel—leather, cracked and well-traveled, with a brass clasp shaped like a crescent moon.

She looked like someone who belonged in a sepia photograph—graceful, slightly out of time, and yet utterly rooted in the moment.

Noah's instinct was to look away, to avoid being seen.

But she was already watching him.

Her eyes met his as she approached—clear, steady, with that unsettling calm of someone who's already read the last page of the book and still wants to discuss the opening chapter.

She stopped a few feet away from him. Smiled gently.

"You came," she said.

Noah blinked. "I—sorry, do we know each other?"

A pause. A faint amusement passed over her expression, not condescending—just... knowing.

"Not yet," she said. "But we will."

Her voice was soft but distinct, like the first crack of sunlight through clouds.

Noah shifted slightly on the bench, caught off guard by her certainty. He tried to reorient himself in logic.

"Did Claire send you? Or—sorry, this is probably weird, I've just had a—long week."

Mira tilted her head slightly, considering him as if he were a question she'd already answered.

"No one sent me," she replied. "And you didn't come here by accident."

That caught him.

He narrowed his eyes. "What do you mean?"

She stepped closer—not invading, but close enough for him to notice that her coat had the faint scent of cedarwood and something like old pages.

"You're at the edge," she said softly. "Of everything you've built to survive. And everything you've refused to feel."

Noah blinked. "Okay... That's poetic, but also—kind of presumptuous?"

A small smile tugged at her lips. "It's not presumption if it's true."

He looked away, uncomfortable, but not angry. Just exposed.

"How do you know my name?" he asked, glancing back at her.

"I didn't say your name," she replied.

His jaw tensed slightly.

"No, but—" He shook his head. "You're playing a game."

She studied him for a moment, then gently placed her satchel on the bench beside him. With quiet ceremony, she unlatched the moon-shaped clasp and reached inside. Her movements were unhurried, like someone leafing through memories.

She pulled out a leather-bound journal and handed it to him.

He stared at it.

The same one.

He'd left it in his apartment.

His mouth went dry.

"How—?"

Mira met his gaze with something gentler than explanation.

"This isn't a book," she said. "It's a doorway. But only if you're ready to stop trying to walk backwards."

Noah didn't touch it.

"You expect me to just... believe all this?"

She didn't answer right away. Instead, she turned and walked a few paces away, her eyes drifting toward the stained-glass window above them.

"People only ask for proof," she said, "when they don't trust their own knowing."

Noah stood, unable to stop himself.

"What are you? Some kind of therapist? Spiritual guide? Is this some curated grief experience? Because honestly, I'm not in the mood for mysticism right now."

Mira turned back to face him. Her eyes weren't offended. They were patient.

"You've mistaken mystery for performance," she said. "They aren't the same."

He hesitated.

"What is this place?"

"Between," she said. "Not where you were. Not yet where you're going."

He looked at the journal again, now resting on the bench like a question.

Mira walked to the edge of the platform and gazed into the distance. A faint sound echoed—a low hum, not quite a train, not quite anything he could name.

"You don't have to understand," she said quietly. "Just don't look away."

He felt something pull in his chest—tight, unfamiliar.

Mira turned to leave. She picked up her satchel but left the journal behind.

"Wait," he called out, unsure why.

She paused, halfway toward the shadowed corridor.

"Why me?"

She looked over her shoulder, the faintest smile tracing her lips.

"You're the one who broke."

And then she was gone.

No footsteps. No door.

Just gone.

Noah stood alone again.

But the silence had changed. It no longer felt like emptiness.

It felt like an invitation.

The journal exchange – "The Law of Release"

Noah stood stiffly by the bench, hands still in his coat pockets, as Mira returned. Her boots made no sound this time. She moved like wind threading through leaves—present, yet evasive. Somehow, she seemed even calmer than before, which only made his nerves bristle more.

She studied him with a quiet, steady gaze. Not judging. Just... witnessing.

"You're still here," she said, almost as if surprised.

"Didn't realize I had somewhere better to be," Noah muttered, kicking lightly at a loose tile near his feet.

Mira smiled faintly. "You think you're stuck. But you're just paused."

He gave a dry laugh. "Is that supposed to be comforting?"

"No," she said. "It's supposed to be true."

He rubbed the back of his neck. His shoulders felt tight, his jaw sore from clenching. "Okay, look. You keep saying these cryptic things like you're auditioning for a dream sequence. But I'm not dreaming. This is real. And real people—real *things*—don't just... show up in empty train stations quoting riddles."

She said nothing for a moment. Then, with the care of someone placing something sacred between them, she unslung the satchel from her shoulder and slowly opened it.

He instinctively leaned closer.

She withdrew the journal with both hands, as if it might break if handled too quickly. The leather looked ancient—dark, worn smooth at the edges, with faint gold embossing across the front. *The Law of Release.*

The moment she revealed it, Noah felt a strange flutter in his chest. It wasn't fear, exactly. It was *recognition*. Like walking into a place you've never been but swearing you've seen it in a dream.

He shook his head and stepped back slightly.

"What is that?"

She held it out to him.

"A mirror," she said. "Of sorts."

He didn't move to take it.

"I've had enough metaphors for one day," he muttered.

Mira's expression didn't change. "You're mistaking stillness for emptiness."

"Oh good," Noah said dryly. "More riddles."

She took a breath—not annoyed, not impatient. Just... steady.

"The universe is always speaking," she said. "But we only hear it when we're still. You've been running from silence so long, you've mistaken noise for guidance."

He flinched slightly at that. Not visibly. But inwardly, something twitched. Like a wire had been plucked.

She took a step closer, the journal still in her hands.

"This," she said, "is not a book of answers. It's a map of the places you refuse to go."

Noah scoffed. "Sounds like a self-help trap."

She tilted her head slightly. "You're more afraid of surrender than of failure."

That hit closer than he wanted.

Noah looked away, into the shadows between the benches. "I don't *need* a journal to tell me I screwed up."

Mira was quiet for a moment. Then she spoke, softer now.

"It's not here to tell you what you already know," she said. "It's here to help you un-know what's been killing you slowly."

He looked back at her, sharply.

"Un-know?"

"Yes," she said. "The lies you've worn like armor. The definitions you've mistaken for truth. The control you've clung to like a raft in a storm that's already passed."

Something in her tone unsettled him—not because it was cold, but because it was *kind*. And it had been a long time since anyone had spoken to him without agenda or expectation.

She stepped forward again, just close enough that the journal was now within his reach.

Noah hesitated.

His fingers twitched.

His rational mind screamed against it—*Don't take the weird book from the strange woman who materializes in train stations.* But curiosity had already rooted itself in his gut. And maybe, just maybe, some small, aching part of him wanted to believe there *was* a reason for all this chaos.

He reached out. Slowly. Lightly.

The moment his fingertips touched the leather, it felt warm. Not temperature-warm—but *alive.* Like it had been waiting for him. Like it *knew.*

He looked at Mira, unsettled. "What is this, really?"

She met his eyes.

"A key," she said. "But you'll only find the door if you stop searching with your eyes."

He opened his mouth to ask another question—

But she was gone.

No footsteps. No rustle of fabric. No parting words.

Just gone.

The station was still. The flickering lantern overhead hummed faintly, but otherwise, silence had reclaimed the space like a tide rushing back in.

Noah turned in a slow circle, heart thudding, mouth dry. "Mira?"

Nothing.

His fingers tightened around the journal. The leather felt heavier now, charged. It pulsed against his palm—not physically, but somehow energetically. Like holding it connected him to something bigger than himself.

He looked down at the cover again.

The Law of Release.

There were no instructions. No subtitle. Just those four words, embossed in a gold that shimmered faintly in the dim light.

He swallowed.

Outside, a distant wind rattled against the station windows. The world, for all its chaos, remained unchanged. But Noah didn't. Not entirely.

He sat back down on the bench, journal resting on his lap like a question.

One he wasn't ready to answer.

But he was holding it now.

And that was a beginning.

Reading the first pages – A door opens

The city outside Noah's apartment pulsed with the soft, uneven heartbeat of late night—distant car horns, the occasional echo of footsteps below, the flicker of a neon sign in the window across the street that blinked *OPEN* even though no one ever seemed to be inside.

Noah lay in bed, eyes wide open, staring at the cracked ceiling like it might spell something out.

Sleep wasn't coming. Not even close.

His phone was facedown on the nightstand. He hadn't touched it in hours. The silence from it was almost more deafening than the noise he'd tried to outrun the past week—coworkers pretending not to see him pack his things, Claire's voice trembling as she said she "needed to find herself," the sound of the door clicking shut behind her.

He sighed and turned onto his side, only to find the journal still sitting on the pillow next to him.

He hadn't meant to bring it into bed. He'd tossed it on the kitchen counter when he got home, then later moved it to the couch, then finally—without thinking—set it beside him like a pet he wasn't sure he trusted.

Now it just sat there, waiting.

Noah stared at it for a long moment. He could almost hear Mira's voice in his head.

"You've mistaken noise for guidance."

He reached for the journal.

It was heavier than he remembered. The leather warm to the touch, the cover soft but firm, like something worn smooth by many hands. There were no markings on the spine, no barcode or publisher's logo—just those four gold-embossed words:

The Law of Release.

He opened it.

The first page was blank, but not emptily so. The paper had a rich, textured feel—like parchment, not printed stock. At the top of the next page, in neat, slanted handwriting, was a single sentence:

"What are you holding that no longer serves you?"

Noah blinked. His fingers tightened slightly on the edge of the page.

What are you holding...

He exhaled. "Where do I even start?"

The next page:

"Most people carry pain like proof. But what if you didn't need to prove anything anymore?"

He swallowed hard.

It was eerie—how much the journal seemed to *know*. Not specifics. But the feeling of being seen without being watched.

He flipped again.

This page was fuller—several lines of handwritten reflection:

"To release is not to lose. It is to choose softness over struggle. To surrender the illusion of control is not weakness—it is wisdom. Ask not 'How do I fix this?' Ask: 'What am I gripping that is already gone?'"

Noah leaned back against the headboard.

Something shifted in his chest—nothing dramatic. Just the faintest ripple in the still water of his denial. He closed the journal for a moment, resting it on his lap.

"This is ridiculous," he muttered. "It's just a book. Probably some underground wellness trend."

But he didn't put it down.

He rubbed his palms over his face, trying to clear the pressure behind his eyes.

A memory surfaced—uninvited.

He was ten years old, sitting cross-legged on the floor of his childhood bedroom, building a Lego city that had taken him three days. His dad had just come home from a long trip, and Noah was eager to show him.

But his father was tired. Frustrated. The city had spilled slightly into the hallway, and without seeing it, he stepped directly into one of the towers.

Plastic exploded everywhere. Red, blue, yellow bricks skittered across the hardwood floor.

His dad sighed. "Noah, you've got to stop leaving things out. Clean it up."

He didn't mean to be cruel. He was just busy. But something lodged in Noah's chest that day—a conviction: *if I want people to stay, I need to control the mess.*

Noah opened his eyes, breath caught in his throat. He hadn't thought of that moment in years.

The journal sat quietly, open again.

Another question:

"Is what you're clinging to still here—or just the fear of what happens if you let go?"

He shut the book quickly.

His heart thudded.

A strange, tight feeling worked its way into his stomach. Not panic. Not grief.

Something older. Raw. Like someone had knocked on a door he'd sealed years ago and somehow walked in anyway.

He stood up and crossed the room, pacing in the dark.

His apartment looked suddenly unfamiliar. The minimal décor, the carefully arranged bookshelf, the color-coded planner on the desk—all things he once took pride in—now felt sterile. Staged.

He glanced at his reflection in the window—blurred by city light, distorted by the flickering neon.

"Who even am I without all this structure?" he whispered.

But no answer came. Just the soft thrum of traffic below and the journal's quiet weight calling from the bed.

He walked back. Picked it up again. This time he didn't read—just held it. Pressed it to his chest like a warmth he hadn't known he needed.

A thought crossed his mind, unbidden and unformed:

Maybe I'm not here to rebuild what I lost.

Maybe the life he had wasn't lost—it was *released.*

And something else... something deeper... was waiting.

Somewhere behind the noise.

Behind the fight.

Behind all the armor.

He laid the journal on his nightstand.

And for the first time in days, sleep came. Not because he found answers.

But because, for a moment, he stopped demanding them.

The symbolism of the station – Was she even real?

The next morning, Noah woke to sunlight struggling through his apartment blinds, a pale golden wash that softened the corners of his small bedroom. For a moment, he lay still, disoriented. Not from sleep—but from the *absence* of the usual heaviness.

The journal was still on his nightstand, its leather cover faintly warm in the light. He didn't touch it, but he *felt* it.

A single question echoed from the night before:

Is what you're clinging to still here—or just the fear of what happens if you let go?

Noah sat up. The city called out like a low hum in the distance, the kind of noise that blurred into your bones if you lived in it long enough. But something within him pulsed with quiet insistence.

The train station.

He hadn't planned to return. It felt absurd even considering it. But the image of Mira—serene, timeless, watching him with eyes that seemed to understand things even *he* didn't—wouldn't let go. She had placed something in his hands, yes. But more than that—she had opened something *in* him.

And now he needed to know: was she real?

Or had he imagined the whole thing?

The walk was longer than he remembered. The night before had been a blur of aching feet and heavy thoughts. Now, in daylight, the city seemed different—too *bright*, too *ordinary*. Glass storefronts reflected traffic. Commuters bustled past, eyes locked on screens. Even the air smelled different—like exhaust and burnt coffee.

Noah turned down a side street, then another, searching for the same winding route he took the previous night. At times, he hesitated, unsure of the exact turns—until he saw it again:

A rusted sign with half-faded letters: **WILLOW STATION**.

It was barely visible behind a tangle of overgrown ivy and chain-link fencing. A narrow path, more dirt than pavement, curved behind an old industrial building, leading to the platform.

But something was wrong.

He stepped onto the platform.

The benches were still there—but covered in layers of dust and leaves, like they hadn't been used in years. The lantern that had flickered warmly the night before was cold and broken. The windows of the station office were boarded up.

The whole place felt... *abandoned.*

Noah turned slowly, heart thudding in his chest.

It was as if time had unraveled overnight. The platform he'd sat on, the space that felt suspended between worlds—now looked forgotten by both.

He stepped forward, half-expecting Mira to reappear, like some archetype conjured by grief and need. But the air was still. The only sound was the caw of a distant crow and the crunch of gravel under his boots.

He looked around for a station master, another passenger, *someone.* But it was empty.

"Excuse me?" he called out, his voice echoing off brick and silence. "Hello?"

No answer.

He found a kiosk near the far end of the platform—its touchscreen dead, its printed schedule curled from weather. Most of the trains listed hadn't run in years. A few notices were still tacked to the bulletin board, yellowed with time.

And then he saw it—barely clinging to a rusty pin at the corner.

A flyer. Torn. Faded. The colors bled with rain and age.

But Mira's name was there.

"Mira Allyn – One Night Only. Spoken Word & Silence: An Evening of Stillness and Sound."

Noah blinked. Pulled the flyer closer. No date. No venue.

Just her name, and beneath it, in faint typewriter font:

"Let go. You're already here."

He stared at it, mouth slightly open, pulse quickening.

Had he imagined her? Had she been a hallucination? A figment of some emotional rupture?

He closed his eyes.

The sensation of her presence returned—not visual, but visceral. The way her voice wrapped around truth like silk. The way her words opened doors inside him he didn't know existed.

Maybe she was real.

Maybe she was *only* real in the way the most important things are—those that slip past logic and lodge themselves in the soul.

As he stood there, something in the air changed. A sudden gust of wind swept across the platform, and for the briefest moment, it smelled of sandalwood and paper. The scent of the journal.

He turned instinctively—but no one was there.

Just sunlight through dust. Silence stretching long.

Noah slowly walked back to the center of the platform. He sat on the same bench, brushing away some leaves, and let his hands rest in his lap.

Maybe the station was more than a place. Maybe Mira *was*, too.

A mirror, she'd said. Of sorts.

He closed his eyes, breathing deeply. The sounds of the city had dulled here—as if this pocket of the world was still holding its breath, waiting.

A door had opened last night.

This place—abandoned, crumbling, barely a memory—*had become sacred* in its own way. Not because of its structure. But because of what it revealed.

Himself.

His resistance.

His longing.

His fracture.

And the faint, flickering whisper of something more: *release.*

Maybe the station didn't need to make sense.

Maybe she didn't either.

He opened his eyes and took out the journal from his satchel. It hadn't left his side. The pages ruffled in the wind, fluttering to a line he hadn't seen before.

"What if the truth comes in disguise—through strangers, through silence, through the spaces between what is and what was?"

Noah closed the book, stood slowly, and turned to leave the station behind.

He didn't know what was waiting ahead. But for the first time, he wasn't trying to force an answer.

Maybe the unknown wasn't a threat.

Maybe it was an invitation.

FIRST ACT OF SURRENDER – OPENING TO THE UNKNOWN

The city stretched below him like a map he no longer knew how to read. Noah stood on the rooftop of his apartment building—thirteen stories above the streetlights, the honking, the blurred faces and purpose-driven bodies of the world he used to feel part of.

The wind was soft but steady, wrapping around him like a presence. It carried the scents of concrete, distant rain, and something faintly floral—like memory.

Behind him, the rooftop garden was a mess of wild plants, untrimmed vines, and neglected flowerbeds. A single bench sat facing the skyline. Rusted. Familiar. He hadn't been up here in over a year. Not since he and Claire shared a bottle of red wine one autumn evening, legs tangled, heads tilted toward stars they couldn't name. That night, he believed in forever.

Now, only the silence remained.

He clutched the journal in both hands. Its leather was worn but alive, like something that had traveled far to meet him.

He hadn't meant to come up here. But something inside him was restless all day—like a tide pulling inward. The station. The flyer. Mira's eyes that seemed to say, *you already know*. None of it made sense, and all of it refused to let go.

He sat on the bench. The metal was cold beneath him.

Above, the sky was streaked in deep navy and pale violet, the last remnants of twilight clinging to the edges. City lights flickered on like stars of another kind. Not celestial. But human. Electrical. Desperate to keep the dark at bay.

Noah opened the journal to a random page.

His fingers paused.

A short passage, handwritten in ink the color of dusk:

"Surrender isn't giving up.

It's giving *in*—

to something wiser than fear,

to the current beneath the surface,

to the life already waiting when you stop fighting."

He read it again, aloud this time, his voice barely above the wind.

"Surrender isn't giving up..."

The words landed somewhere deep in his chest, as if his body remembered them long before his mind ever read them.

He exhaled, shaky.

All this time, he'd thought letting go meant losing control. And control was the only thing that kept him from falling apart. Or so he believed.

But what if the real fracture wasn't in the letting go—but in the gripping?

What if the fall *was* the healing?

His eyes stung suddenly. No sobs. No breakdown.

Just a soft, unexpected warmth behind the eyes, like water welling up after too long frozen.

He closed the journal and held it against his chest.

There were no answers tonight. No plan. Just this rooftop. This wind. This open sky.

And within him, the first quiet opening.

A crack.

A whisper.

A breath of something not broken, but *brave*.

Noah looked up, and in his mind, he spoke to her—not Mira exactly, but the part of her that had shown up in the quiet places of his soul.

"I don't know what I'm doing," he whispered. "But okay."

The wind wrapped around him like a response.

Not reassurance.

Not clarity.

But *presence*.

He stood.

For a moment, he thought of throwing the journal into the sky. Letting it fly. But he didn't. Not yet.

Instead, he turned to face the city—still unfamiliar, still full of noise—and stepped closer to the edge of the rooftop.

Below, headlights moved like fireflies. People lived lives he would never know.

But above, the first stars had appeared.

He didn't move.

He just stood there, still.

Breathing.

Listening.

And somewhere inside him, the long-held grip of resistance began to loosen.

Something had begun.

Something real.

And it started—not with a roar.

But with a whisper.

PART 3: THE MIRROR OF RESISTANCE

Opening the first lesson – "What are you resisting?"

Rain whispered against the window like a voice too gentle to ignore. Gray light sifted through the blinds of Noah's apartment, casting lines across the hardwood floor, the couch still indented from a restless sleep. A mug of black coffee sat cooling on the windowsill, untouched.

Noah sat cross-legged on the floor, the journal resting in his lap.

This time, he hadn't reached for it by accident. There was no trance, no sleepwalking curiosity. He *chose* to open it. Something had shifted since the night on the rooftop—a tremor, not an earthquake. But real enough to bring him here, back to these pages that unnerved and intrigued him.

He ran his fingers over the cover again. Leather, worn at the edges. The scent reminded him of old libraries and distant storms. He exhaled slowly, then opened it to the first full page marked *Lesson One*.

At the center of the page, written in bold, imperfect ink:

"What are you resisting?"

He stared at the question.

It didn't blink.

Didn't soften.

Didn't offer context or comfort.

Just five words. But they echoed louder than any sentence he'd read in years.

Noah leaned back against the couch, the leather creaking beneath his shoulder blades. He traced the letters with his eyes again. *What are you resisting?*

At first, his mind tried to respond with sarcasm.

Everything, he thought.

I'm resisting being broke. I'm resisting heartbreak. I'm resisting your damn question.

He set the journal down beside him and picked up his coffee. It tasted bitter, lukewarm. He took one sip and set it back down, staring out the rain-streaked window. The city beyond was blurred—gray on gray, water washing the outlines of buildings into nothing.

But the question had already landed somewhere deeper than the surface.

What are you resisting?

A flicker of memory came unbidden.

He saw himself at twenty-four, standing outside his father's house in the freezing dark, holding a duffel bag. His father had just told him—again—that dreams didn't pay rent. That "real men" took jobs they didn't love. That being a creator was just another way to run from responsibility.

That night, Noah left. He didn't look back.

But he remembered the heat in his chest. Not passion. Not bravery.

Defiance.

Even now, a decade later, that heat hadn't entirely cooled. He'd told himself he was chasing something better—success, stability, status. But under all of it had been a need to prove something. *That he wasn't weak. That he was enough. That he was right.*

And now?

Now that job was gone. The office he'd once ruled with confident presentations and tight deadlines was empty without him. Claire, who had seen both his tenderness and his armor, was gone too—slipping away long before she ever said the words.

Noah pulled the journal back onto his lap.

He turned the page. Below the question, more handwriting appeared, less bold but no less clear:

"Resistance wears many masks: anger, avoidance, perfection, numbness, control.

To see your resistance is to see the cage you've built to protect yourself. It served a purpose once. But does it still?"

His throat tightened.

He flipped to the next page. There, in smaller script, was a list:

- What truth have you avoided facing?
- What emotion have you shoved down and renamed "strength"?
- What silence are you filling with noise?
- What did you once love that you no longer allow yourself to want?

He stared at the list until the questions started to blur. His body felt warm, unsettled.

No. Not now.

Too much.

He closed the journal and stood abruptly, nearly knocking over the coffee. He paced to the kitchen, opened the fridge. Closed it. No appetite.

His thoughts swarmed.

What am I resisting?

Not knowing. Not being in control. Not feeling like a failure. Needing anyone. Forgiving myself.

He rubbed his eyes, hard. Something inside him wanted to push the journal far away—toss it in a drawer, bury it under laundry, pretend it never appeared. But another part... that part from the rooftop... was still listening.

He dropped onto the couch, groaning as he let his head fall back.

Another memory came.

Claire, sitting across from him at the edge of their bed. Her eyes were red. Her voice was calm but tired.

"You never let me in, Noah. Not *really*. Everything's fine until it's not. You don't fall apart—you *shut down*. And I'm done trying to guess what's behind the walls."

He remembered biting his tongue, resisting the urge to argue.

Because she wasn't wrong.

He had always prided himself on being composed. Reliable. Unshakable. He handled pressure. He met expectations. He excelled.

But maybe that was the mask. Maybe his real face was beneath the mask he forgot he was wearing.

Noah opened the journal again.

At the bottom of the page, the ink faded into a final invitation:

"Just write. Even if it's messy. Especially if it is."

He got up and retrieved a pen from the kitchen drawer.

Returned to the couch. Sat cross-legged again.

The journal trembled slightly in his hands, or maybe it was just him.

On the next blank page, he wrote:

"What am I resisting?"

And then paused.

He tapped the pen once. Twice. Ten times.

Minutes passed.

Finally, in small, careful letters, he wrote:

"I'm resisting being seen.

I'm resisting feeling lost.

I'm resisting slowing down.

I'm resisting admitting I don't know who I am without the things I used to cling to.

I'm resisting grieving.

I'm resisting starting over.

I'm resisting forgiving my father.

I'm resisting needing anyone.

I'm resisting failure.

I'm resisting... being soft."

He stared at the last line.

That one wasn't planned. It just came.

Being soft.

That was it, wasn't it? The armor, the ambition, the control—it was all designed to keep him hard, polished, untouchable.

Because softness had once been punished. Or misunderstood. Or mocked.

But here, in this quiet apartment with only the rain and this strange book, his softness had found its voice again.

It hadn't spoken in years.

And now it whispered:

What if the strength you seek is hidden inside the softness you fear?

Noah didn't know what to do with that voice yet. But he didn't silence it.

He just let it echo.

And for the first time in a long time, he didn't try to fix, answer, or overcome it.

He just... listened.

He closed the journal gently and set it beside him.

The rain kept tapping the window, patient and rhythmic.

The silence wasn't empty anymore.

It felt like a beginning.

The reflection exercise – Confronting the inner dialogue

The journal sat open on Noah's kitchen table, a pool of soft morning light stretching across the pages like a silent invitation. He hadn't meant to open it again so soon—had even told himself last night that he needed a break from its haunting truths.

But it pulled at him.

Like a thread unraveling.

This morning's page was titled simply:

"List the top 5 lies you tell yourself."

No context. No soft landing. Just the challenge—blunt and surgical.

Noah sat with a bowl of oatmeal slowly congealing in front of him, spoon untouched. He reread the line. Again. And again.

His first instinct was to roll his eyes.

"Top 5 lies?" What was this—therapy via middle-school journal prompts?

But beneath the sarcasm was something else.

Discomfort.

He tapped the side of the bowl with the spoon. Counted the taps.

Five lies. How hard could that be?

He picked up the pen.

And sat there.

And sat there.

Until finally, one word formed at the top of the page.

1. "I'm fine."

Noah's pen hovered. He underlined it. Then again.

"I'm fine."

How many times had he said those two words like armor? How many times had he used them as a wall?

He closed his eyes.

A memory flickered.

He was ten. Sitting in the back seat of his mother's car, tears drying on his cheeks. His teacher had pulled him aside after class to say he "got distracted too easily," that "he needed to try harder like the other boys." That she'd be calling home.

His mother gripped the steering wheel tighter than necessary as they drove. Silence clung to the space between them like static. Finally, she asked:

"Why can't you just *focus*, Noah? You're smarter than this. What's wrong with you?"

He remembered wanting to scream. Wanting to cry again.

But instead, he'd whispered, "I'm fine."

Even then, it was a cover. A way to survive. A way to keep her disappointment from cutting any deeper.

He shook the memory off and moved to the next line.

2. "I don't need anyone."

This lie came slower, like a confession carved out of stone.

It had kept him warm during lonely nights. Had justified silence when friends reached out and he never texted back. It had been the script in his mind every time Claire offered to carry his burdens and he pushed her away.

"You don't need to worry about me."

"I've got it handled."

"I don't want to be a burden."

"I'm fine." (Again.)

But under all of that was the aching truth: he *did* need people. He just didn't know how to hold need without shame.

His father had never needed anyone. That's what he used to say.

"You take care of yourself, son. No one's going to do it for you."

Noah once believed that made him strong. Now it just made him tired.

3. "If I'm not perfect, I'll be forgotten."

This one made his stomach turn.

He wrote it slowly, every letter dragging across the paper like resistance embodied.

He remembered a school talent show. Eighth grade. He'd practiced his piano piece for weeks, convinced he'd win the prize for "Most Outstanding Performance."

He hit a wrong note in the second half. Just one.

The applause afterward was polite. He smiled, bowed. But when the winner was announced, it wasn't him.

His mother had smiled tightly in the car on the way home.

"Next time, don't get distracted. People only remember the ones who get it right."

It was a small comment.

But it burrowed deep.

Ever since then, Noah had equated visibility with perfection. Love with performance. If he didn't nail the project, the pitch, the partner role—he feared vanishing. Irrelevant. Replaceable.

Claire had once said, teasing:

"You're like a lighthouse. Always standing tall, but I don't know if you ever let anyone see *inside*."

And he'd smiled and brushed it off.

But now...

Now the echo hurt.

4. "Success will fix everything."

He stared at this one for a while.

It wasn't something he'd ever *said* out loud.

But it was the motor behind everything.

The overtime. The sacrifices. The missed birthdays. The unspoken apologies.

His career had become a ladder he climbed to escape a burning house. Every promotion was supposed to silence the old voices. Every bonus a balm to the scar that said he wasn't enough.

He had told himself that if he just *got there*, the rest would resolve itself.

But here he was. At the bottom of what was supposed to be the peak. Fired. Alone.

And nothing had been fixed.

5. "It's too late to change."

This lie tasted like rust. Like old metal kept in the mouth too long.

He wrote it and his hand shook slightly.

He was thirty-four. Not old. Not young.

But the idea of starting over? Of letting go of everything he built just to chase something undefined?

That terrified him.

He remembered walking past a small art shop near the station a few weeks ago. He'd stopped at the window. Inside, a woman was painting—a canvas alive with color and wildness.

Noah had once loved drawing.

Sketchpads filled his teenage room.

But somewhere along the way, he told himself that art was indulgent. That he had to be realistic.

"Grow up," his father had said once, catching him doodling instead of studying. "You're not going to survive on that nonsense."

And so he had folded that part of himself up and buried it.

Now, he could barely remember what it felt like to create for the sake of creation.

He stared down at the five lines.

"I'm fine."

"I don't need anyone."

"If I'm not perfect, I'll be forgotten."

"Success will fix everything."

"It's too late to change."

They looked like tombstones now. Each one marking a part of himself he'd silenced, suppressed, or sacrificed.

And yet, there was something sacred in seeing them written.

In naming them, they lost a little power. Like ghosts seen in daylight.

He turned the page. More handwriting met him there:

"You can't release what you refuse to name.

Truth is not always a light—it is often a mirror.

But if you're brave enough to look, it can become a doorway."

Noah sat back in the chair. The kitchen was silent, save for the soft hum of the refrigerator and the distant rhythm of rain against glass.

He closed his eyes and whispered the lie again:

"I'm fine."

Then shook his head gently.

"No... I'm not."

It wasn't shameful.

It was human.

And for the first time, that felt like enough.

The mirror as a symbol – Literal and figurative

The bedroom was quiet. Too quiet.

Noah stood still in the doorway, journal in hand, as if unsure whether to enter. The sun had long gone down, but he hadn't turned on the overhead light. Only a small lamp in the corner glowed—its amber halo soft and forgiving. The air smelled faintly of rain and the detergent he'd used on his sheets earlier that afternoon. A kind of hollow cleanness. Too sterile to feel lived in.

He stepped inside.

The mirror stood tall against the far wall, angled slightly toward the bed. It was one of those full-length pieces Claire had insisted on buying when they moved in together. "Everyone needs a mirror that lets them see their whole self," she had said, winking at him. He remembered rolling his eyes at the time, teasing her about her Pinterest addiction. But secretly, he liked it.

Until recently, he'd only ever used it in passing—checking that his collar sat flat or his belt matched his shoes. Quick glances. Utility. He never lingered. Never looked *through* it.

Tonight, he pulled the chair from his writing desk and placed it directly in front of the mirror. The move felt ceremonial. Like taking a seat before something sacred—or dangerous.

He lowered himself slowly into the chair, the journal resting on his lap.

His reflection stared back.

For a long while, he just looked.

Dim light pooled around him, creating deep shadows under his cheekbones and around his eyes. The man in the mirror looked worn. Thinner. Tired in a way that went beyond sleep. The kind of tired that accumulated from years of pretending.

He reached up, touched his jaw, then traced the lines at the corners of his mouth. His fingers moved as though mapping something unfamiliar. It startled him—how foreign he looked when he really paid attention.

"Look at yourself as if meeting you for the first time."

The journal's line echoed in his mind.

He tried.

What would a stranger see?

Someone thoughtful, maybe. Serious. Intelligent.

But also... sad. That was what struck him the most.

There was sadness etched into the slope of his shoulders, the way he held his mouth tight like he was afraid it might fall open and spill something he couldn't take back.

He exhaled slowly.

Then spoke into the quiet.

"I'm fine."

The words dropped from his mouth like a default setting. Lifeless. Reflexive.

He met his own eyes in the mirror.

Then, almost involuntarily, the truth emerged beneath it.

"I'm terrified I'll never matter."

His voice cracked.

He swallowed, hard.

The silence afterward was deafening—thick with everything that had been unsaid for years.

He reached for the pen tucked inside the journal and wrote the two lines on a blank page.

Lie: I'm fine.

Truth: I'm terrified I'll never matter.

He looked back at the mirror.

"I don't need anyone."

Pause. A shaky breath.

"I'm afraid if someone really saw me, they'd leave."

He wrote that one too.

Lie: I don't need anyone.

Truth: I'm afraid if someone really saw me, they'd leave.

The mirror didn't flinch. Didn't judge. It simply held him.

His reflection now looked different—not physically, but energetically. Like something had softened in the tension of his brow. His eyes, once dulled, shimmered faintly. With recognition. With pain. With something that could almost be... grace.

A faint memory surfaced—of being a child standing on tiptoe in his parents' bathroom, watching himself practice a speech for the school assembly. He remembered how earnestly he had smiled at his reflection then, mouthing each line with bright-eyed belief.

That boy had believed he could change the world.

He had believed *he* mattered.

Noah stared into his own face and wondered when that boy had disappeared. When the mirror stopped being a window and became a wall.

He lifted his hand again, this time pressing his palm against the cold glass. The reflection mimicked him, but something about the act felt... different. Sacred, even. Like touching another version of himself trapped on the other side.

"It's too late to change," he whispered.

His hand trembled against the glass.

"But maybe that's not true."

He waited, as if the mirror might respond.

And in a way, it did.

He saw not the man who had failed.

But the man who had *survived*.

Not the one who'd lost his job or been left behind.

But the one who was still here. Still trying. Still breathing.

The mirror shimmered slightly as he leaned forward, forehead nearly touching the glass.

A tear slipped down his cheek. Then another.

It wasn't a breakdown. Not quite. But it was real.

Raw.

Holy.

He closed the journal with care and placed it gently beside him. The candle on his nightstand flickered from a draft, throwing light and shadow across the room.

For a moment, Noah sat completely still.

He wasn't fine.

He wasn't unbreakable.

But maybe—just maybe—he was finding something more powerful than perfection.

Maybe he was beginning to wake up.

From behind the veil of years and performance and armor.

And in the mirror's quiet reflection, he could finally see himself—not as a failure.

But as someone worthy of forgiveness.

Of softness.

Of truth.

He stood slowly, turned off the lamp, and walked to the window. Outside, the city blinked its tired lights into the dark sky.

Noah whispered to the glass—just as he had to the mirror.

"Okay."

It wasn't an answer.

It was a surrender.

And maybe that was the point.

Emotional rebellion – Resistance fighting back

The slam of the apartment door echoed down the corridor, louder than Noah expected.

His breath fumed in the chill night air, fogging around his face as he stormed down the steps and out into the street. He didn't bother grabbing a coat. The cold bit at his skin, but he welcomed it. He *wanted* to feel something sharp, something physical, something that could cut through the storm inside his head.

The journal.

The mirror.

The truths he'd spoken aloud.

It had been too much. Like a dam cracking open just enough to remind him there was an ocean waiting behind it.

His footsteps slapped hard against the wet pavement as he walked. Fast. No destination. No plan. Just motion. Just escape.

What the hell am I doing?

The question throbbed in his mind, over and over like a heartbeat.

This is crazy. It's all crazy. A stranger at a train station hands me a journal, and now I'm sitting in front of mirrors like I'm in a therapy commercial. What's next? Crystals and spirit animals? Chanting in the woods?

He turned a corner without thinking, nearly tripping over a busted curb. Somewhere, in the tangle of his thoughts, a deeper voice murmured that he was scared. But he shoved it down, hard.

This isn't clarity—it's collapse. This is what a breakdown looks like.

He kept walking. Faster.

The city felt alien. Off. Even the streetlights seemed too bright, too knowing. He passed a couple laughing at a corner café and felt a sudden surge of bitterness rise in his chest. *How do they just... function? Smile like nothing is wrong?*

He hated them for it.

He hated himself more.

He reached a familiar intersection, one he used to pass every morning on the way to the office. The little grocery on the corner, the same mural of jazz musicians on the wall, faded from years of sun and weather. And then, without meaning to, his feet brought him to the one place he hadn't visited in months:

The old diner.

"Benny's Breakfast Bar." Open 24/7, serving the best hash browns this side of nowhere.

It had been a ritual spot once. Sunday brunches with Claire. Late-night strategy chats with coworkers during product launches. Comfort food and fluorescent lighting. A place where everything felt ordinary.

And standing outside the smudged glass door, he almost turned away.

But then he heard the voice.

"Noah?"

He froze.

He knew that voice.

Turning, he saw a man step out from the diner's door—tall, broad-shouldered, with a well-worn hoodie and the same sideways grin that hadn't changed in a decade.

Eli.

His college roommate.

"Man, I *thought* that was you," Eli said, pulling him into a casual half-hug. "Dude, where the hell've you been?"

Noah gave a hollow laugh. "Oh, you know. Around."

"You look like you've been dragged backwards through a philosophy class and a hurricane."

"Sounds about right."

Eli chuckled and motioned toward the diner. "Grab a coffee? I was just about to head out, but I've got time."

Noah hesitated.

But his hands were numb and his thoughts louder than ever. Coffee couldn't hurt.

Inside, the booth was sticky in all the familiar ways. A waitress refilled their cups without asking, and the hum of an old jukebox played something Motown and moody in the background.

Eli took a sip, leaned back. "So. What's going on?"

Noah stared at his coffee.

"You ever feel like your life isn't yours anymore?" he said finally. "Like you've been performing the same script for so long, you forgot it was even a role?"

Eli raised an eyebrow. "Whoa. That's... deep for 10 p.m."

"Sorry," Noah muttered.

"No, no. I get it. I mean, to a point. I fake it all the time. Work's a mess, my relationship's hanging by a thread. But, you know—what can you do?"

Noah glanced up.

There it was.

That shrug. That tired smile. That *resigned acceptance.*

The same one Noah had worn for years.

Something about seeing it on Eli—a mirror of his *old* self—made his stomach churn.

"You ever think maybe we're not supposed to keep faking it?" Noah asked.

Eli blinked. "Not sure we've got a choice, man. Life's life. You grind, you hustle, you pretend. Everyone does."

Noah shook his head slowly. "Maybe that's the problem."

Eli snorted. "Sounds like you've been reading one of those self-help books. What was it—'The Power of Now' or whatever?"

Close, Noah thought.

He almost mentioned the journal. Almost brought up Mira. Almost asked Eli if he ever felt like life was trying to tell him something—if he only knew how to listen.

But the words died in his throat.

This wasn't the moment.

And Eli wasn't the one.

As they left the diner, Eli clapped him on the back. "Whatever storm you're in, just keep your head down, yeah? Push through. That's what we do."

Noah smiled weakly. "Yeah. Sure."

But as he walked away, down another unfamiliar street under another flickering streetlamp, the storm inside swelled again.

His stomach twisted.

His thoughts rebelled.

What if he's right? What if this is all just temporary insanity?

He remembered the mirror. The truths he'd spoken.

He remembered how his voice had trembled. How his chest had cracked open.

And now, he wanted to take it all back.

To delete the words. To shut the journal. To pretend it hadn't happened.

He wanted to scroll through Instagram, drink something strong, rewatch an old sitcom and drown everything out in laugh tracks and neon colors.

Resistance had returned—with a vengeance.

His inner voice mocked him.

So you had a moment. Big deal. You think a couple journal prompts and some poetic stranger are going to fix you? Wake up. You're broken. You've always been broken.

He squeezed his eyes shut.

Stop.

His fists clenched.

Enough.

He stood still on the sidewalk, barely breathing, as headlights passed by in the distance.

The weight of it all crushed down.

But somewhere, in the back of his mind, a quieter voice spoke up.

It didn't yell. It didn't argue.

It simply said:

This is what resistance looks like. Don't run.

Noah didn't know if he believed it yet.

But for the first time in hours, he didn't walk away from the thought.

He stood still. In the cold. In the dark.

And let the storm rage without trying to silence it.

The breaking thought – "Maybe I'm not the enemy"

The apartment greeted him with stillness.

No music. No screens flickering. Just the hush of a city gone to sleep and the soft tick of the wall clock like a heartbeat he could almost mistake for his own.

Noah dropped his keys on the counter with a sound that felt too sharp. Too final. His shoes stayed on as he walked slowly to the living room, then lowered himself to the floor like gravity had finally claimed him in full.

He sat there.

Not thinking.

Not moving.

Just... being.

The journal lay on the table, untouched since that morning. Its worn leather cover caught the soft spill of streetlight through the window, casting long shadows across the rug.

He stared at it for a long time.

Then, without knowing why, he reached for it. Held it in both hands like something fragile, sacred.

It felt warm from the sun that had touched it earlier, or maybe that was his imagination. Maybe everything lately had been his imagination.

He ran a thumb along the edge, hesitated, then pressed it to his chest.

Eyes closed.

"I don't know who I am anymore."

The words left his mouth before he could stop them. A whisper. Not desperate, not angry—just honest. Clean.

It hung in the air like breath in winter.

And for a moment, something inside him softened. Gently, tentatively. Like ice beginning to melt under the first rays of spring light.

There was no flood of clarity.

No booming voice from above.

Just a flicker.

A flicker of something unfamiliar.

Kindness.

Toward himself.

He wasn't sure where it came from—maybe the exhaustion, or the conversation with Eli, or the mirror he couldn't unsee. Maybe the ache in his chest that had grown too loud to ignore.

But in that stillness, with the city sleeping and the journal pressed close, something shifted.

Not pity.

Not self-congratulation.

Something else.

He opened the journal with slow, deliberate fingers, turning past the scribbled thoughts and questions that had haunted him the past few days.

A new page awaited him.

A different kind of page.

At the top, in careful handwriting, were the words:

"You are not your resistance.
You are the one observing it."
He read it once.

Twice.

Then again, softer this time, as if reading it to a child.

You are not your resistance.

You are the one observing it.

A quiet breath left his lungs. He hadn't realized he'd been holding it.

For so long, he had *fused* with the storm inside him. Believed it was *him*—the anger, the doubt, the perfectionism, the constant self-correction. He had built an identity around holding it all together, performing, proving, pushing. And every time it cracked, he thought it was *him* breaking.

But what if... that wasn't true?

What if the voice that screamed, *You're not enough, You're lost, You're failing*—wasn't the truth of him?

What if that voice was only fear?

Only habit?

What if beneath the noise, there was something quieter, wiser... watching?

Noah let the thought linger.

A slow, warm swell began in his chest. Gentle. Not euphoria, not bliss—just warmth. Like someone had opened a window after months of stale air.

He leaned his head back against the couch, tears gathering behind his eyes without falling.

He didn't need to know who he was right now.

He didn't need to fix everything.

He just needed to stop fighting himself long enough to listen.

To notice.

To observe.

And maybe—just maybe—to offer himself the same compassion he'd given to strangers. To Claire. To coworkers and baristas and neighbors and everyone else he'd bent over backward to please.

Maybe the person most deserving of his gentleness... was him.

He rested the journal on his knees, his fingertips grazing the margin where someone—Mira, perhaps—had scrawled a tiny note in the corner:

"Sunlight doesn't force the flower to open. It waits, and it warms."

Noah closed his eyes.

Let the words wrap around him.

Let the flicker glow a little brighter.

This wasn't a victory.

It wasn't a full surrender.

But it was *something*.

A breath he hadn't taken in years.

A moment of stillness where he could be... just himself.

No armor.

No answers.

Just the beginning of something real.

And maybe, for now, that was enough.

THE WALLS BEGIN TO CRACK – HOPE IN HONESTY

Noah sat cross-legged on the living room floor, the journal open in front of him like a letter he'd been avoiding reading. The soft hum of the refrigerator and the distant whoosh of a car on wet pavement were the only sounds in the apartment.

The list stared back at him—familiar, sharp, undeniable.

The Lies.

1. *I'm fine.*
2. *I don't need anyone.*
3. *If I'm not perfect, I'll be forgotten.*
4. *I deserve this pain.*

5. *I have to earn love.*

He exhaled slowly, the kind of breath that felt like an apology.
To himself.
To the boy he once was.
To the man he had become pretending he didn't need to feel anything at all.
He reached for a pen.
Not with the same defiance from before.
But with something gentler.
Tentative, still unsure.
But real.
He began to write.

1. *I'm fine.*
   → **I'm hurting. And that's okay.**
2. *I don't need anyone.*
   → **I've always wanted connection—I'm just afraid I don't deserve it.**
3. *If I'm not perfect, I'll be forgotten.*
   → **I am loved for who I am, not what I prove.**
4. *I deserve this pain.*
   → **No. I deserve healing, grace, and space to grow.**
5. *I have to earn love.*
   → **Love is not earned. It's allowed. And I'm learning to allow it.**

He stared at the truths for a long time.
They felt foreign.
And fragile.
But also... *true.*
Not in a performative way, not like something he was trying to convince himself of.

But like something he had always known and just forgotten how to say out loud.

His hand hovered below the list, as if waiting for permission from somewhere inside.

And then, in clean, slow handwriting, he wrote one more line:

"This is not the end of me. This is the beginning of meeting myself."

He blinked.

Sat with it.

Then, carefully, gently, closed the journal.

The apartment felt quieter now.

Not empty—*still.*

Like the silence that follows a long overdue truth.

He carried the journal with him to the bedroom, setting it down beside his pillow like a companion, not a burden.

Noah slid beneath the covers, the weight of the day settling around him like a thick but breathable quilt. He didn't check his phone. Didn't rehearse conversations in his head. Didn't spiral.

Just... breathed.

As sleep began to pull him under, a dream bloomed, unannounced and warm.

He was eight, maybe nine.

In the sunroom of his childhood home, where the light streamed in golden through gauzy curtains. A quiet afternoon. No noise. Just him and a canvas.

He was painting.

A sky, wide and blue, with impossibly soft clouds drifting like thoughts he didn't need to chase.

His mother was humming faintly in the kitchen, the scent of lemon tea curling through the air.

He didn't know about deadlines. Or heartbreak. Or pressure to be anything other than himself.

He just painted.

Free.

Smiling.

Whole.

The boy looked up—right at him. Not startled. Just calm. As if he'd been waiting.

And when he smiled, it wasn't with pity or nostalgia.

It was welcome.

As if to say, *Come home. I've saved your place.*

Noah stirred softly in sleep, his hand grazing the journal by his side.

Outside, the wind moved gently through the trees.

Inside, the wall didn't fall.

But it cracked.

And through that slender crack, the faintest light began to glow.

Quiet.

Warm.

Hopeful.

Like the beginning of something honest.

PART 4: THE WEIGHT OF CONTROL

– A Journal Entry Leads to a Name – Julian

Morning came in on a hush of pale blue, the light diffusing softly through the apartment windows like it was trying not to wake anything too suddenly. Noah sat at the small dining table, the journal open before him. A chipped ceramic mug of black coffee steamed beside him, untouched, forgotten.

His pen scratched lightly against the paper.

No performance. No perfection. Just truth.

He copied the truths from the night before into a new page, rewriting them not to reinforce but to remember.

"This is not the end of me. This is the beginning of meeting myself."

He underlined it slowly. Twice.

There was a warmth in his chest he hadn't recognized in weeks. Maybe months. Not joy, not yet—but an easing. Like something heavy had unclenched. He wasn't whole, not by any stretch. But he was *present*.

And for the first time in a long time, that felt like enough.

He flipped to the next page of the journal, half-curious, half-afraid of what he'd find. The handwriting was the same—elegant, looping—but the tone of the prompt carried a different weight.

"Revisit a part of yourself hidden behind someone you used to know."

His brow furrowed. He read it again.

Immediately, like a ghost called by name, a face formed in his mind.
Julian.

Julian Reed.

A grin lit Noah's lips before he even realized it. Not
performative—reflexive. *Real.*

Julian was...

Chaos and clarity.

Loud music and late-night walks.

Poetry scribbled on diner napkins. Conversations that tunneled
straight into the marrow of your soul and never left it quite the same.

They had met in college. Roommates, randomly assigned, and yet
somehow it had felt cosmic. Like a collision written long before either
of them had arrived.

Julian had been wild in the best way. Not reckless—but unbound.
He said things like "truth is a dance, not a destination," and had a habit
of quoting Rilke in casual conversation. He didn't believe in resumes,
only resonance. Believed that you didn't *become* someone—you
uncovered yourself, like layers peeled back to reveal the light you were
born holding.

And Noah?

He had admired him.

And envied him.

And, for a short while, let himself be pulled into that orbit of
fearlessness.

But eventually, the tides of adulthood had demanded structure.
Certainty. Control.

And one day, without a fight, without even a goodbye, they'd
simply... drifted.

Noah swallowed hard and reached for his phone.

His thumb hovered over the keyboard.

What do you even say to someone who knew your soul before you'd
built all these walls?

Still, he typed.

"Julian. Hey. It's Noah. Been a long time. Just wanted to say... I've been thinking about you."

He stared at it.

Then, without overthinking, he hit send.

The message left a strange ache in his chest, like dropping a letter into the ocean and hoping it might still find a shore.

He set the phone face down on the table and pushed the journal slightly away, running his fingers through his hair.

And then it buzzed.

He flinched, heart hitching.

A reply.

He turned the phone over.

Julian: *"Been thinking of you too. Let's meet."*

Three words, and a floodgate cracked open.

Noah sat back in his chair.

He wasn't sure if it was relief or fear rushing through him.

But he texted back.

"When?"

Julian: *"Today. If you're free. Same place we used to go. Diner on 8th. You still take your coffee with too much sugar?"*

Noah smiled. Actually smiled.

"Some things never change," he wrote.

"Some things do," Julian replied.

"That's the point."

Noah closed the journal slowly, as if it were something sacred.

Then, for the first time in years, he walked out the door not to fix anything, not to perform, not to escape—

But to remember who he used to be.

And maybe, just maybe, to reclaim him.

– The Café Reunion – The Ghost of Who He Was

Rain whispered against the windows like an old friend keeping secrets. The café on 8th hadn't changed. Still painted in hues of amber and deep teal, with mismatched chairs, crooked bookshelves, and candles in mason jars flickering on each table. A barista with lavender-dyed hair hummed along to the soft strums of a live guitar player in the corner, his fingers plucking a melancholic tune that bled into the quiet chatter and the scent of cinnamon and coffee beans.

Noah stood just inside the doorway, scanning the room. For a moment, he wondered if Julian would show. Not because he doubted the reply, but because this place felt like a portal to a life that no longer existed. Like he was stepping into an old photograph of himself—one that smiled without effort.

He took a seat at a small round table by the window. The wood was nicked with initials and pen scratches, but the candlelight made it feel like the center of something timeless. He ordered coffee—two sugars, just like always—and tried to still the nerves vibrating beneath his skin.

He heard the door open behind him. The little bell chimed.

Noah didn't turn around right away. He didn't have to.

Julian's energy arrived before he did.

"Some things really don't change," came a familiar voice. Playful. Calm. Intrinsically comfortable in its own skin.

Noah looked up.

Julian was somehow exactly the same and completely different. Still tall and lean with a wild edge to his curls, dressed in layered textures—gray wool, worn leather, a scarf that looked more like art than clothing. A messenger bag slung across his chest, a paint stain on his jeans, a spark in his eyes that hadn't dimmed.

"Julian." Noah stood, unsure if he should shake his hand or hug him.

Julian answered the hesitation for him, pulling him into a firm, unpretentious hug.

"Damn," he said as they sat down. "You look like someone pressed you out of a spreadsheet."

Noah laughed despite himself, smoothing the front of his jacket. "I'll take that as a compliment."

"Take it as a wake-up call." Julian grinned and signaled the barista. "Two coffees. Make his exactly how he likes it—dangerously sweet."

The barista nodded knowingly. "Already did."

Julian turned back to Noah. "She remembers. The Café Gods are still on your side."

There was a brief silence as they looked at each other. The moment stretched. Noah could feel it—an invisible current, threading back through years of absence, friendship, and unspoken things.

"How long's it been?" Noah asked.

Julian shrugged. "I stopped counting when the world stopped making sense. Somewhere between heartbreak number four and artistic crisis number seven."

Noah smiled, but it felt tight. "You look good."

"I feel messy," Julian said. "But in a way that finally makes sense."

Their coffees arrived, steam curling up like quiet offerings between them.

"And you?" Julian sipped. "Still building empires?"

Noah hesitated. His fingers curled around the mug. "I... was. Until two weeks ago. Lost the job. Lost... a lot, actually."

Julian leaned back. He didn't say anything at first. Just nodded, his gaze softening.

"So, the dam broke."

Noah blinked. "What?"

"I always figured you were walking around with pressure in your chest like a glass jar about to shatter." Julian stirred his coffee, thoughtful. "You used to be wild, man. When did you start needing everything nailed down?"

The question landed like a fist to the ribs.

Noah opened his mouth to answer, but nothing came out. He stared at the table. His fingers tapped the side of the mug as if trying to find rhythm in the chaos of his thoughts.

Julian let the silence sit.

"You remember that night junior year," Noah said finally, voice quiet, "when we walked to the river at 2 a.m. and you made that stupid toast about 'freedom being the art of letting go before the fall'?"

Julian grinned. "I was drunk on cheap wine and Bukowski."

"Yeah. But I remember thinking..." Noah trailed off.

"Thinking what?"

"That I didn't believe it," he admitted. "Even then. I pretended to. But I needed something to hold onto. Structure. Control. Something."

Julian's eyes didn't leave his. "And what's that gotten you?"

Noah let out a bitter laugh. "A resume. An apartment that's too clean. A relationship that walked out the second I wasn't impressive anymore."

Julian's expression softened. "That wasn't about you not being impressive. That was about you not being *you*."

That landed harder than Noah wanted it to. He looked out the window. Rain dripped down the glass like slow tears.

"Why now?" Julian asked gently. "Why reach out after all this time?"

Noah exhaled. He pulled the journal from his coat and set it on the table like a secret too heavy to keep in his pocket.

Julian raised an eyebrow. "Looks ancient. What is it?"

"Something someone gave me. A stranger. Sort of." He paused. "It's called *The Law of Release.*"

Julian leaned in. "Sounds like the opposite of everything you ever stood for."

"I know," Noah said, almost smiling. "And yet... it's doing something to me."

Julian's gaze rested on him, deep and unflinching. "Or maybe it's *undoing* something. Something you needed undone."

Noah didn't reply. His throat was tight. His chest heavier than before—but not in a bad way. More like he'd finally stopped holding his breath.

"Do you ever feel like you built your whole life around the version of yourself other people admired?" he asked.

Julian nodded slowly. "Sure. And I've burned that version down more than once. But the ashes always tell me who I actually am."

A pause.

"Maybe that's where you are now, Noah. In the ashes."

The words settled between them like smoke, quiet and undeniable.

They sat like that for a long time, coffee cooling, rain falling, and guitar strings humming like the heartbeat of something unspoken.

Noah glanced down at the journal.

"I think I'm ready to read the next page."

Julian smiled, slow and knowing.

"Then don't read it alone."

– The Confession – The Moment Noah Broke Away from Himself

The café light dimmed as a cloud passed over the street, muting the afternoon into a kind of cinematic hush. The guitar player in the corner shifted to a jazzier tune, his fingers dancing without urgency. Julian was still mid-sentence, but Noah wasn't hearing the words anymore.

Something had cracked open.

It started with the sound of the rain—how it fell in a rhythm that reminded him of something—no, *somewhere*. A rehearsal room. Concrete floors. The hum of amps and the metallic sting of guitar strings. He remembered the warm buzz of old speakers and the thrill of hearing his own voice echo back at him, raw and alive.

And then he was there.

The summer after graduation.

The windows in the old rehearsal studio were cracked open to the thick July air. Heat soaked the floorboards, and Noah's shirt clung to his back. He stood barefoot in the center of the room, a guitar slung low across his body, fingers calloused from days of playing until his wrists ached. Beside him sat a worn notebook of lyrics, half-formed, mostly crossed out, but alive with something *real*.

Julian sat on the amp, barefoot too, thumbing through a poetry zine they found at a sidewalk fair. "You know we're going to do this, right?" he said between lines. "We're going to play that open mic next month and change someone's life."

Noah smiled without looking up. "Just one person?"

Julian grinned. "Gotta start small. Then we'll build a cult."

A laugh, light and effortless. There was something sacred in those moments—the freedom to dream without needing a roadmap.

Noah strummed a few chords. He was working on a melody that sounded like thunder wrapped in glass. It was unfinished. Everything was unfinished.

Then his phone buzzed.

He checked it. A message from Rachel.

"They offered you the job. Six figures. Full benefits. Starts in two weeks."

Noah's fingers stopped moving. The chord dissolved into silence.

Julian glanced up. "What's that look?"

Noah swallowed. "The consulting firm. They want me."

Julian whistled. "Damn. That was fast."

Noah didn't reply.

Julian set the zine down. "You're not actually considering it, are you?"

"I don't know." But he did. He felt the decision calcify the moment he read the message. Felt it press against his ribs like obligation.

Julian leaned forward, his expression soft but piercing. "You said you wanted to give it a year. One year to just *be an artist*. Try the music. Write the stuff that scares you. Live lean. You promised yourself."

Noah ran a hand through his hair, pacing. "Yeah, but maybe I was being naive. My dad already thinks I've wasted too much time. Rachel wants to move in next fall. She said this job's a sign that things are falling into place."

Julian's jaw tensed. "Falling into *place*, or falling into line?"

Noah didn't answer. The guitar strap felt heavier now, like it belonged to someone else.

Julian stepped off the amp. "I'm not trying to guilt you. You gotta do what you gotta do. But... just don't lie to yourself while you're doing it."

Noah looked away, out the cracked window where the sun bled over rooftops like spilled paint.

"I don't want to disappoint anyone," he murmured.

Julian's voice was low. "What about disappointing *you?*"

Silence.

In the weeks that followed, Noah took the job.

He packed up his music gear. Sold the amp. Boxed the lyrics. Bought button-downs and sensible shoes. Told himself it was a phase, that he'd come back to it later. But the later never came.

The door to that part of himself didn't slam shut—it just... quietly faded, like a song left unfinished.

Back in the café, the weight of that moment hit Noah like a wave returning from deep water. It stole the breath from his chest and left behind something raw and exposed.

Julian must've seen it in his face.

"What just happened?" he asked gently.

Noah didn't look up right away. His voice came out hushed, like it might shatter.

"I remember the moment I walked away from myself," he said.

Julian didn't interrupt.

Noah's fingers traced the rim of his cup. "I traded freedom for certainty. And I've been losing pieces of myself ever since."

A long pause.

Julian let the words hang in the air, the way good friends do—with reverence.

Then, softly, he said, "It's not too late, you know."

Noah looked up, eyes wet but clear. "To do what?"

"To remember who you were before the world told you who to be."

Outside, the rain was still falling. But inside, something else was beginning.

Not quite forgiveness.

Not quite healing.

But a first return to the place he left behind.

– The Illusion of Control – Julian's Insight

The rain had stopped by the time they stepped out of the café, but the air still smelled of wet pavement and spilled espresso. Streetlights flickered on, halos of amber melting into the early evening fog. The world seemed quieter now, as if holding its breath while Noah and Julian walked side by side, their conversation stretching past the edge of comfort.

Noah had his hands shoved in his coat pockets, eyes on the sidewalk. Julian walked with that same untamed ease he always had, the kind of presence that made people feel seen but not scrutinized. He wasn't in a hurry. He never had been.

They paused at the corner where a bookstore's display window gleamed with poetry anthologies and faded first editions. Julian tilted his head toward it, as if the books themselves might chime in on the conversation.

"Control," he said quietly, "is like a dam. You think it's keeping the chaos out. But all it's doing is holding everything *in*—all the fear, grief, anger. You can't keep it up forever. Something cracks. And when it breaks, man... you're not walking away dry."

Noah scoffed, trying to turn it into a laugh. "Yeah, well, I'd rather drown in structure than chaos."

Julian chuckled, not unkindly. "Thing is, it's not one or the other. Structure's not bad. But when you use it to build a prison instead of a shelter, you forget there's a whole sky out there."

Noah leaned against the edge of a lamppost. "So you're telling me surrendering is the answer? That I should just stop trying to steer anything?"

"No," Julian said, shrugging. "I'm saying maybe it's not about steering at all. Maybe it's about learning how to *float.*"

The word landed like a stone in Noah's chest.

Float.

It sounded reckless.

It also sounded like freedom.

Noah looked out at the cars moving in slow rows, their headlights slicing the dusk into strips. The world never stopped moving. Not for anyone.

"You make it sound easy," he muttered.

Julian's face softened. "It wasn't."

They stood in silence for a beat too long. Then Julian shifted, pulling a weathered ring from his thumb and slipping it into his pocket. "You remember Maya?"

Noah blinked. "Your girlfriend from back in the day? The painter?"

"Yeah. We were engaged."

Noah's mouth fell slightly open. "I didn't know that."

"Most people didn't," Julian said, his voice low. "It fell apart right before the book deal did. Two losses, back-to-back. I was gutted. I tried to hold it all together, act like I was in control. Told everyone I was fine. You know that one."

Noah nodded, too quickly.

"But pretending you're not breaking doesn't make the cracks disappear," Julian continued. "I lost my voice for almost a year. Couldn't write anything real. Everything felt like a lie. I even convinced myself it was better to just... stop."

He looked over, eyes lit with a mix of memory and something more—something like hard-earned grace.

"But here's the thing," he said, "when everything I'd built collapsed, I thought it meant I was weak. A failure. But the truth is, the life I had was never mine to begin with. It was built on fear. On trying to prove something. Control was my armor. It looked strong—but it kept me from *feeling* anything."

Noah exhaled slowly. The wind picked up, scattering leaves across the sidewalk like loose thoughts.

Julian continued, his tone gentler now. "The only way out was to stop fighting. To let go. And that's when the words came back. That's when *I* came back."

Noah stared at the streetlight above them. It buzzed faintly, casting long shadows over the cracks in the pavement.

"Letting go sounds like a luxury," he said finally. "Some of us can't afford to collapse."

"You're already collapsing," Julian said, not cruelly, but like someone pointing to smoke where Noah had refused to see fire. "You just keep doing it in secret. Quiet breakdowns no one's allowed to name."

That one hit.

Noah looked away, throat tight. "I don't know who I am without control," he whispered.

Julian stepped closer, hands in his coat pockets. "That's okay. Maybe the point isn't to know. Maybe it's to *meet* yourself."

Noah blinked against the sting behind his eyes.

"Come on," Julian said, nodding toward the park. "Let's walk a little more. It's almost blue hour."

They moved quietly beneath the trees, branches clicking above like old typewriter keys. Noah didn't speak for several blocks. His thoughts were too full, a tangle of resistance and longing.

Control had been his compass.

His shield.

His god.

But what if it was also his cage?

When they finally reached the curve of the river, Julian turned to him with a grin.

"You'll hate this, but I'll say it anyway," he said.

"Oh God, what?"

Julian tilted his head. "Surrender isn't giving up. It's giving *in*—to something wiser than fear."

Noah laughed through his nose. "Yeah, I *do* hate that."

Julian slapped his shoulder. "Told you."

They stood by the water in silence, the city behind them, the future somewhere just out of frame. Julian lit a cigarette. Noah didn't ask for one.

And though he didn't say it aloud, somewhere in the mess of his mind, a question lingered like a small, steady flame:

What if I've been holding on to the wrong thing?

When they parted ways, Noah walked slower than usual. Each step felt unsteady, like a man walking after months in a cast.

He didn't know if he believed in surrender yet.

But for the first time, he didn't entirely *disbelieve* it either.

– The Walk Home – Control Revealed as Fear

The night had thickened around Noah like a wet coat, heavy and clinging. As he stepped away from the café and Julian's parting grin, the city's noise surged back into his ears—horns blaring, the shriek of a bus's brakes, footsteps slapping sidewalks slick with mist. Everything moved fast. Everyone moved forward.

Except him.

Noah shoved his hands deep into his coat pockets, shoulders hunched as if trying to disappear into the folds of himself. Julian's voice echoed in his mind, soft but persistent: *"You're already collapsing. You just keep doing it in secret. Quiet breakdowns no one's allowed to name."*

He hated how true that felt.

Each step stirred old thoughts. Half-formed memories surfaced like flotsam after a shipwreck—moments he'd long buried beneath ambition and neatly made plans.

There was that time he'd stayed late at the office, working through the night on a project no one would remember, while outside his window the sun had risen over a park where children played. He'd barely noticed.

There was the dinner party where someone asked about his music—and he'd lied, said he hadn't played in years because it was "just a phase." He'd laughed it off while his throat tightened, and his fingers ached for the feel of strings.

And then, a sharper memory: his father's voice after his first big job offer. "Finally," he'd said. "Something real. Something that'll last."

Noah had nodded and smiled. Inside, something had curled into itself like a dying flame.

He passed a street vendor now, packing up unsold pretzels and hot dogs, whistling to himself. There was something peaceful in the man's rhythm, unhurried and indifferent to the world's grind. Noah kept moving, trying to hold himself together.

But the city wouldn't let him.

It pressed in—cars honking, people shouting into phones, bright lights flickering like overloaded circuits. The weight of it matched the storm gathering inside him. He turned a corner and stumbled into a construction site partially cordoned off by sagging orange mesh.

He paused.

There, beneath the harsh fluorescent bulbs, a wrecking crew was at work. A mechanical arm swung against the side of an old brick building, and with each hit, parts of the wall caved inward. Chunks of plaster and stone fell to the ground with a kind of hollow finality.

Boom.

Crash.

Dust rising like ghosts.

Noah stood still, transfixed. The machine paused, repositioned. Another swing. Another collapse. The wall, once solid and proud, was giving up its secrets—layer by layer.

He felt a strange kinship with it.

How many times had he reinforced his own walls? With plans, with productivity, with polite smiles? How many times had he ignored the cracks? Pretended nothing was shifting, even as parts of himself quietly dislodged and crumbled?

He watched a piece of the wall fall—a clean break. It split in two, then shattered against the ground.

And in the echo of that sound, he felt it.

The truth.

Control wasn't strength.

It never had been.

It was fear, cleverly disguised—wearing tailored suits and calendar blocks and tight-lipped nods. It had masqueraded as confidence, as certainty, but really, it had been his hiding place. His prison. And he had kept himself locked in, clutching the keys like they were trophies.

He leaned against the nearby scaffolding, breath catching in his chest.

"I'm so tired..." he whispered, almost not recognizing his own voice. "I'm so tired of needing to hold it all together."

The wind picked up, tugging at his coat.

"I'm tired of being scared," he added, quieter now.

Noah closed his eyes. In the darkness behind his lids, he saw flashes—him as a kid, humming to himself as he painted dinosaurs on his bedroom walls. Him in college, barefoot on the grass, laughing with Julian, playing chords under the stars. Him in that tiny studio apartment, writing poems he never showed anyone.

All those pieces. Still in there. Buried, but alive.

He opened his eyes to the crumbling wall again, the exposed beams, the hollowed-out heart of what once stood tall.

And he didn't feel shame.

He felt permission.

To fall apart, yes. But also... to rebuild.

He turned slowly from the site, his breath steaming in the cold air. The city moved around him, oblivious. But something in him had shifted. Something small and quiet. Something that could no longer be undone.

Maybe Julian was right.

Maybe surrender wasn't defeat.

Maybe it was the first step toward freedom.

He pulled the journal from his coat pocket and held it against his chest as he walked. Not as a shield this time—but as something closer to a compass.

And for the first time in a long while, he didn't rush home. He let his pace slow. He let the city blur. He let himself *feel*.

Each step forward was uncertain, yes—but it was his.

And somewhere, beneath all the rubble, Noah felt the stirring of a self he hadn't met yet.

Not the man who controlled everything.

But the one learning to *let go*.

– A New Page in the Journal – A Decision to Loosen the Grip

The apartment was dim when Noah returned, but not cold. Something about the silence felt different this time—less like isolation, more like a held breath finally let go.

He slipped off his shoes, dropped his bag on the couch without caring where it landed. The usual reflex to tidy, to straighten, to *fix*—it didn't rise. He walked barefoot to the kitchen, poured a glass of water, and stood in the quiet hum of the refrigerator, the condensation cool against his palm.

He sipped slowly. Then, without even thinking, he reached for the journal.

The leather was soft in his hands, worn now with frequent use. He sat cross-legged on the floor, the coffee table pushed slightly askew in front of him. The lamp glowed low beside him, casting long shadows across the woodgrain.

He flipped open to the next page.

There, in that same deliberate, imperfect handwriting:

"You can't heal while bracing for impact."

He stared at the words.

Read them again.

And again.

And they undid him.

Because all this time—years, maybe decades—he had been tensed. Shoulders locked. Jaw clenched. Preparing for failure, rejection, abandonment. Bracing for pain before it could find him. Holding every emotion like a soldier holds his weapon.

He put the journal down beside him, opened to that page, and grabbed a pen. His hands were steady now.

He wrote:

"I controlled everything so I wouldn't feel the pain.

But the control became the pain.

It built walls too thick to breathe through.

And now I'm tired.

And I want to feel again."

He paused.

Then, one more line:

"Maybe it's okay if I don't know what comes next."

He let the pen rest on the open page and exhaled. The kind of exhale that comes from deep inside the ribs. The kind that takes effort. The kind that makes room.

Noah leaned back against the edge of the couch, eyes fluttering shut. For the first time in years, he didn't reach for his phone. No checking messages. No replying to emails. No social scroll to drown his thoughts.

He stood slowly and moved through the apartment, switching off lights until only the bedroom lamp remained. He looked around the room—dishes in the sink, unfolded laundry in a basket, a painting half-finished leaning against the wall. A mess.

His mess.

And somehow, it didn't feel like failure. It felt like life.

He walked to his record player and pulled out a vinyl—an old one. Dusty, cracked at the corners. Something soulful and unpolished. He placed the needle gently on the spinning black and waited for the crackle.

Then came the music—low, raw, real. The kind that held emotion in every imperfection.

And then, without needing a reason, the tears came.

Soft, quiet. Not like a storm—like a release.

He let them.

No apologies. No shame. No explaining it to himself or anyone else.

Just tears.

He stood by the window, resting his hand on the cool glass. Outside, the city buzzed on—traffic lights blinking, someone laughing down the street, a car alarm briefly whining before falling silent.

He cracked the window open and let the night air roll in. It was sharp and clean and alive with possibilities.

The curtains swayed slightly in the breeze.

Something in him swayed, too.

He wasn't fixed.

He wasn't finished.

But he had loosened his grip.

And in that loosening, there was something new: space.

For breath.

For music.

For truth.

Noah closed his eyes and whispered, not to anyone, not even to himself—just to the night:

"Okay."

It wasn't a declaration.

It wasn't even a promise.

It was permission.

And it was enough.

PART 5: THE POWER OF SURRENDER

Exhausted from Effort – A Call to Stillness

Noah awoke slowly, as if surfacing from a long dive through something deeper than sleep.

His body ached—not from strain, but from something more elusive. As though every cell had carried too much for too long. The sheets were twisted around his legs, and his pillow damp in the corner where his cheek had pressed against it.

For a long moment, he didn't move.

The apartment was still.

Not just quiet—*still*. Like the air had settled into prayer.

Light streamed faintly through the blinds, filtering into the room in golden-gray streaks. Dust floated lazily through the beams like soft particles of thought. Somewhere in the distance, a dog barked once. Then nothing again.

Noah blinked toward the nightstand.

The journal lay open. He didn't remember leaving it that way. But then, he didn't remember much after the tears, the music, and the whisper to the window.

His eyes caught on something scrawled near the bottom of the page—different ink than before, darker. It must have always been there, but now, it glowed as if underlined by fate:

"There is more wisdom in your breath than in your mind."

Noah read it again, the words working their way into him like a warm tide. His breath, slow and full, moved through his chest with surprising ease. For the first time in a long time, he noticed it. Not controlled. Not braced. Just... happening.

A deep inhale.

A longer exhale.

The body, remembering itself.

And in that silence, something shifted.

Not a sound exactly—more like a presence.

He felt it before he heard anything. A quiet knowing. An invisible tether pulled gently at the base of his spine. His eyes drifted toward the door.

A soft knock. Once. Then again.

Noah sat up. The air tingled.

Barefoot, he padded across the cool floor, heart thrumming quietly but not in panic—in anticipation. He opened the door slowly.

There she was.

Mira.

Just as she had appeared at the station—unfazed by time or logic. Dressed simply, with that same serene gravity, as if the world moved differently around her. Her eyes held something endless. Not answers. Not riddles. Just depth.

She smiled, small and knowing.

"You've been carrying a war inside you," she said. "It's time to lay it down."

Noah swallowed, unsure if he should speak or nod or question the reality of her presence. He did none of those. He just stepped back slightly, as if to invite her in.

But Mira didn't move forward. She turned instead, motioning gently.

"Come with me," she said. "It's time."

He looked down at his shirt—wrinkled from sleep. His hair messy. The apartment unkempt.

"But... I'm not ready," he began.

"You don't have to be," she said. "That's the point."

He hesitated a moment longer, then something within him softened—like the loosening of a knot. He reached for nothing. Grabbed nothing. Just stepped out, barefoot, into the hallway, and followed.

They walked without speaking.

Down stairwells, through quiet streets, past the rising scent of morning rain on warm pavement. The city hadn't fully woken. It was the in-between hour—where time feels slightly bent, like anything is possible and nothing is urgent.

Noah wanted to ask questions. Where were they going? Why now? How did she find him?

But something in her presence answered all of it without a word.

They turned onto a path he'd never noticed before. A narrow alley framed by ivy-covered walls and a quiet hum beneath his feet—like the ground was alive and listening.

At the end of the path, a door. Not to a building. Not quite to anything he could label.

Mira placed her hand gently on it, and it opened.

Inside: stillness.

Not silence. *Stillness.*

The kind that wraps around the soul. That stops the inner noise.

A small, circular room bathed in natural light, with cushions on the floor, a low table, and windows that seemed to open into nowhere and everywhere at once.

Mira gestured for him to sit.

He did.

And for a while, they just breathed.

Nothing was taught.

Nothing was explained.

Nothing was done.

Just breath.

In.

Out.

The forgotten rhythm of being.

Noah's eyes fluttered shut at one point, and for the first time, it wasn't to escape. It was to enter.

In that soft, sacred space, his thoughts slowed—not stopped, but no longer clinging to each other in desperate loops.

He felt his shoulders drop.

His jaw unclench.

His heart whisper: *thank you.*

And when he opened his eyes again, Mira was no longer across from him.

He looked around, startled—but only for a second. There was no panic in her absence. Just quiet. Just space. Just breath.

On the cushion where she'd sat, a single folded piece of parchment.

He picked it up, hands steady, breath slow. Unfolded it.

One line:

"Surrender is not giving up. It's letting go of the fight against what already is."

He held the note to his chest.

And for the first time in his adult life, Noah felt completely still—not empty, not numb, not defeated.

Just still.

The way a forest feels after snowfall.

The way a heart sounds after it stops screaming.

The way a soul begins again.

And from that stillness, something stirred—not effort, not ambition, not strategy.

Something softer.

Something like... life.

And in that quiet place, Noah whispered to no one and everyone: "I'm listening."

The Sanctuary – A Place Out of Time

Mira led Noah down a narrow alleyway, so quiet that even his footsteps felt muffled against the cool, cracked cobblestones. The air smelled of earth and rain, with the distant hum of the city growing more and more faint as they walked. The world, it seemed, was shrinking around him—his mind still spinning from the events of the past few days, the walls of his apartment, the intense conversation with Julian—but here, everything was softening, becoming a quiet blur.

She guided him through a worn wooden door that creaked open with the gentleness of an old friend. The hinges hardly groaned, as if the space beyond had been waiting just for him.

Noah stepped into a room so unlike any he'd known, he almost believed he'd stumbled into another dimension. The air was heavy with the scent of burning sage, the kind that seemed to seep into your skin, making everything else smell faintly of warmth and grounding. Soft cushions in varying sizes were scattered across the floor, inviting relaxation. Green vines clung to the walls, draping down in natural curtains that let muted sunlight filter through.

A single candle flickered on a low wooden table, its flame dancing quietly as if caught in a secret rhythm. The room was dim, the light soft and golden—almost as though time here had forgotten how to rush. There were no clocks. No ticking. Just a flow of energy that felt as though it had always been here.

It was a sanctuary.

Mira didn't speak. She simply gestured for him to sit, and Noah obeyed instinctively, lowering himself onto a cushion, his body sinking gently into its softness. His mind, however, remained restless—a jumble of thoughts and questions—but the room around him, bathed in this quiet reverence, seemed to have a different sort of invitation.

"You're tired," Mira said, her voice low but not forced. It was a statement, not a question, as though she could hear the exhaustion beneath the surface of his words. "You've thought your way into exhaustion. Now, feel your way into surrender."

Her voice was neither commanding nor coaxing. It was simply true, a mirror of the space he'd wandered into. There was nothing to hold onto here, nothing to fix. Just... release.

Noah looked around at the space again, slowly letting it seep in. The lush plants, the soft light, the intimate silence that filled the room as if it were cocooned away from the rest of the world. He felt both small and expansive at the same time, like a child in a dream where the edges of reality were blurry, undefined.

"Lie down," Mira said after a moment. She motioned toward the floor, where the cushions were arranged, inviting surrender. She didn't need to say anything more. Her presence was enough. Her energy, somehow, made him trust that this place held no judgment.

With a quiet exhale, Noah stretched out on the floor, the coolness of the stone beneath him grounding him in a way that felt unfamiliar but profoundly necessary. He closed his eyes. The world outside no longer mattered.

The stillness around him felt different now. Not empty. Not hollow. But full in its silence, as though it was holding him without needing anything in return. He could feel his breath moving through his body, slow and steady, pulling him deeper into a calmness he hadn't known in years.

Mira's presence drifted beside him, and though she said nothing more, her energy wrapped itself around him like a soft, unseen blanket. She was there but not there. Watching, yes, but also allowing him to simply be.

For the first time in as long as he could remember, Noah didn't feel the need to *do* anything. No problem to solve. No goal to reach. Just... being.

And in that space, his breath deepened. His chest expanded, and then it fell. A tiny release. A brief flicker of warmth. The tightness in his chest, which had been a constant companion, began to loosen, inch by inch.

There was something sacred in this room. Something ancient.

Something that had nothing to do with the outside world—no noise, no expectations, no urgency. Just... the simple act of surrender.

And in this act, Noah felt something shift within him. Something that hadn't been there before. A feeling he didn't know how to name, but it settled over him like a soft cloud.

He wasn't alone. He wasn't abandoned. He was simply held—by the room, by the air, by Mira's quiet presence.

And as his body softened, sinking further into the floor, Noah allowed himself to release. To *feel* instead of think.

The world outside could wait. He was finally home.

Breathwork – The Body Unlocks the Soul

Mira sat beside him, her presence as steady and constant as the earth beneath him. She didn't speak right away. The silence was comfortable, filled with a kind of waiting, as if the room itself were holding its breath for what would come next.

"Close your eyes," Mira's voice was soft but unhurried, a gentle current of sound flowing around him. "Let the world fade away. Let your breath be the only thing you hold onto."

Noah hesitated. His chest felt heavy, the air too thick. He was so used to being in control, to the pace of his thoughts, to the weight of his worries. The idea of letting go, of simply being with the breath, felt alien, like trying to step into water when you've spent a lifetime on dry land.

"Slow inhale," Mira guided him, her tone rhythmic and soothing. "Slow exhale. Let your lungs fill, and then release. Gently."

Noah obeyed, his breath shallow at first, tentative. He could feel the tightness in his chest, the muscles reluctant to let go. His mind buzzed with thoughts—too many thoughts. The clutter of his life, his fears, his confusion—it all swirled around him, loud and insistent.

But Mira remained silent, patient, her energy wrapping around him like a soft blanket, never pushing, never demanding. Just *being*.

"Now," she whispered, barely audible, "deeper. Deeper breaths. Let the air fill you, all the way down. Feel it. Feel the rise and fall of your body."

Noah inhaled, deeper this time, feeling the coolness of the air as it entered his lungs, filling them in slow, deliberate breaths. His exhale was just as slow, and for a moment, he felt a tremor ripple through him, like something was stirring beneath the surface.

"Good," Mira's voice was warm, like sunlight. "Now, breathe in a circle. No end. No beginning. Just the flow."

Her words guided him into a rhythm, circular, endless. He began to follow the pulse of the breath, slowly at first, then more deeply. His chest rose and fell with a steady cadence, the breath becoming more pronounced, more full. His body began to release the tension, piece by piece. But still, his thoughts raged. The noise in his head didn't cease, even as the rhythm of the breath anchored him to the present moment.

Then, a shift—a subtle one—like the first crack in ice. His chest began to feel warm, almost alive, and the air around him seemed to thicken. His breath grew deeper, fuller, like the body was reaching for something buried within. His throat tightened, then released, and tears began to well in his eyes.

The tears came without warning, without permission. They were slow at first, unsure, like a rain cloud gathering in the distance. And then—once they began—they wouldn't stop.

Memories flooded in—fragments, flashes—too fast to catch, but they came with a power he couldn't understand. He was back in his childhood home. The sound of his mother's voice, soft but strained. His father, always distant, always calculating. A boy, small and unsure, hiding behind a door, afraid of being too much, too loud, too *there*.

He could feel it all—the weight of his own shame, the unspoken expectations, the tightness in his chest that had never loosened. He could feel the boy he once was, the dreams he buried, the fear he never acknowledged.

The sobs came harder now, wracking through his body with a force he didn't know he could still feel. His ribs trembled with each breath, the tightness in his chest now unraveling, piece by piece, like an old rope loosening its knots. He was gasping, choking on the air as it left him, but it didn't feel bad. It felt like release, like coming home to a part of himself he had long forgotten.

Through the waves of emotion, Mira's voice was steady, like the still center of a storm. "You are safe," she whispered, her voice low and soothing, wrapping around him like a balm. "Let go. Let the breath carry you."

His body felt like it was humming now, vibrating with the deep, primal rhythm of life itself. The energy in his chest, once trapped, now coursed through him—alive, moving, flowing. It was as if his entire being had woken up, as if the breath was unlocking something deeper than just his lungs. It was unlocking his soul.

The tears were endless, raw, and yet, with every sob, the release felt more complete, more sacred. There was a tenderness now, a softness in his chest, like the breath had cleared away the layers of pain and fear that had built up over the years. With every inhale, he felt the pain dissolve, like the tide washing away the shore.

Noah breathed in deeply again, this time slower, more deliberate. The room felt still, as if the entire universe were holding its breath along with him. The sobs began to subside, replaced with a calm that felt foreign, but welcome. His breath had slowed, no longer frantic but steady—strong, even. The vibration in his chest was still there, but now it was soothing, like the quiet hum of a distant song. He let the stillness wash over him, not pushing it away, just feeling it, letting it settle deep into his bones.

Mira sat beside him, her presence solid but gentle. She didn't speak. She didn't need to. The silence between them was full—full of everything that had been released, everything that had been uncovered. The room, now calm, seemed to pulse with a sacred energy that wrapped itself around him, filling the spaces where the pain once lived.

He breathed again—deeply, slowly, peacefully—his body relaxed now, his mind quiet. And for the first time in years, Noah felt something he hadn't allowed himself to feel: *freedom.*

Silence – The Deepest Truth Emerges Without Words

The room was still, the air rich with the scent of sage and something soft—like velvet in the space between breaths. Mira sat beside him, her presence as quiet as the moonlight spilling through the window, her eyes closed, her breathing gentle and steady. There were no more words, no more guidance. Just the two of them, sitting in the vastness of silence, the kind that wasn't empty but full—full of something unspoken, something ancient.

Noah was still, too, as though frozen in time. His body felt heavy but not with fatigue—more like it had been set down into something deeper, like a stone sinking into the softest, most welcoming earth. He didn't know how long they had been sitting this way. Time had lost its grip on him, the ticking of the world outside muffled, distant. All he could feel was the space around him, stretching and breathing in harmony with his own rhythm.

The silence wasn't oppressive. It didn't demand anything from him. Instead, it held him. It cradled him in its quiet, offering him something he had never known before: peace.

At first, there was only the sound of his breath, slow and steady. But soon, the sound of his heartbeat followed, rhythmic and constant. It was a quiet symphony, the music of his own body—alive, present. For the first time in a long time, he could hear it clearly. And then, a deeper sensation—like the silence itself was pressing in on him, but not in a suffocating way. It was as though the silence had become something alive, a living presence that was pulling him into a greater awareness.

He wanted to label it, to understand it, but it eluded him. It wasn't a thought, not really. It was an understanding—deep, innate, not spoken but felt. And then, like a whisper on the edges of his mind, a line from the journal came to him, unbidden, a truth that hung in the air like a delicate thread:

"What you cannot control, you can bless."

The words rippled through him, like the faintest breeze that stirred the surface of water. *Bless,* he thought. It was such a small word, yet it held so much weight in that moment. The power wasn't in the fixing, the fighting, the striving. It was in the letting go, in the surrender. He didn't need to control everything, to grip every moment, every outcome with the fierceness of fear. The need to *figure it out,* to have all the answers, dissolved like mist in the sun.

Noah felt the tightness in his chest release, like a valve opening and allowing the pressure to flow out. His shoulders, which had been rigid and burdened for so long, dropped gently, like a curtain falling in a quiet room. The weight of his jaw, which had clenched tight in tension, loosened. The muscles in his neck, which had been taught with years of stress and control, finally relaxed, stretching out into the stillness. The tension that had wrapped around his body, his heart, his mind, faded into nothingness, as if the silence had taken it all away, piece by piece.

The truth wasn't loud, wasn't a sudden realization that struck him like a lightning bolt. It was soft, subtle, and infinitely more powerful than any answer he could have found through his own striving. He didn't have to know everything. He didn't have to hold onto the world with clenched fists. There was power in allowing things to unfold, in releasing the need to fix everything.

His breath became deeper, more natural, as if his body was now finally breathing with the rhythm of the earth. His eyes fluttered closed, the weight of them gentle, as though everything he had carried had been released, and he could simply *be*.

In that silence, he wasn't alone. He felt connected—connected to the room, to Mira, to the air, to the gentle hum of the city beyond the window. It was as though the silence had woven him into the fabric of everything. The boundaries between him and the world blurred. He was both part of the stillness and the stillness itself. And for the first time, he didn't feel the need to break it, to analyze it, to find something in it. He simply let it be.

In that moment, he understood. *This*—the quiet, the stillness—was not something to fear. It was not emptiness, but wholeness. It wasn't absence, but presence. He had spent so much of his life trying to control, trying to make sense of things, trying to force his world into a shape that felt safe. But this—this freedom in the surrender, in the quiet—was where the answers had always been. Not in the effort. Not in the doing.

In the stillness, he felt the shift in his soul. It was subtle, like the softest of winds, but it was there—unmistakable. His heart, once clenched in a cage of control, was now open, soft, vulnerable, and free.

Mira's quiet presence beside him seemed to confirm it, as if she, too, had been waiting for him to come to this realization on his own, without words, without force. Just *being*.

Noah opened his eyes, and the world didn't seem as loud anymore. It didn't seem as heavy. The questions, the worries, the need for control—they were still there, but they didn't carry the same weight. He felt lighter, like he had stepped into a new version of himself, one that didn't need to *fix* anything, one that could simply *be*.

The silence stretched, long and deep, holding them both in its embrace, and for the first time in Noah's life, he knew that it was enough.

Conversation Without Words – Mira's Gift

Mira reached into the folds of her soft, flowing shawl and pulled out a small object, cupped delicately in her palm. It was a smooth stone, cool to the touch, with a slight shimmer beneath its surface. She placed it gently into Noah's hand, her fingers brushing his skin with a quiet, knowing touch.

Noah looked down at the stone, his thumb tracing the faint patterns that danced across its surface. The stone felt ancient, as though it had carried a thousand stories in its silent weight. He felt the impulse to ask, to demand some kind of explanation, but the stillness of the room, the stillness within him, kept his words at bay.

He looked up at Mira, his brow furrowing slightly. "How do you know what I need?" he asked, his voice barely more than a whisper, afraid that too many words would shatter the calm between them.

Mira met his gaze. Her eyes, deep and steady, seemed to hold all the answers, all the understanding, without needing to say a single word. She studied him for a long moment, as if seeing him for the first time and, at the same time, as though she had known him forever.

"I've walked the path of resistance," she said softly, her voice as gentle as the wind. "I just remembered how to rest."

Her words settled into the space between them, profound in their simplicity. Noah's breath caught in his chest, the weight of the truth settling in. He thought of all the ways he had fought against life—against himself, against the unknown—and how, in doing so, he had only created more distance from the peace he had so desperately sought. The stone in his hand seemed to pulse with the quiet rhythm of this understanding.

Mira's hand then moved to his chest, gently resting over his heart. There was no pressure, no expectation—just the quiet assurance that she was there, that she saw him. Her touch was warm, grounding, and Noah felt something shift inside him—a softening, a breaking open, as though his heart, once so tightly bound by fear and control, was now allowed to breathe freely.

In that moment, it was as if time itself paused, holding its breath. He didn't feel broken. Not anymore. Not here. Not with Mira. He felt something else entirely: held. The sensation wasn't one of repair, but of acceptance. Of being seen, not as a collection of flaws to be fixed, but as a whole being—perfect in its imperfection.

Her hand remained on his heart, and Noah exhaled slowly, as though letting go of the years of tension he had been carrying without even realizing it. The weight of it, of everything he had clung to, melted away, leaving him lighter than he had ever felt.

Mira's eyes locked with his once more, and there was no judgment there, only warmth. Only quiet understanding. She didn't speak again, but in the space between them, the message was clear: this was just the beginning. The beginning of a new way of being. A way of *being* rather than *doing*.

The stone in Noah's hand had become a symbol—not of a future to be controlled or shaped, but of the stillness he could now carry within himself. It was a reminder that he didn't have to fight, didn't have to struggle to earn his place in the world. He could rest. He could surrender. And in that surrender, there would be strength.

Mira stood slowly, her movements graceful and unhurried. She nodded toward the door, an invitation to follow. Noah didn't know what awaited him, but for the first time, he felt no fear in the unknown. He stood, the stone still warm in his hand, and walked with her toward the next step—whatever it might be.

No words were needed. Not now. They were both walking the same path, one that didn't require answers—only presence. Only trust.

Walking Home – Lightness for the First Time

Noah stepped out into the cool night, the air crisp against his skin. Mira had vanished, as quietly as she had appeared, leaving him standing in the shadow of the dimly lit street corner. It felt as though she had never been there—except for the lingering sense of something unspoken, something profound, still reverberating in the space around him.

As he began to walk, there was a slight weight to his steps, not the heaviness of his usual burdens, but a weight born of something lighter, something more substantial. He noticed his feet touching the ground with an awareness that felt new, each step soft but sure. He slowed his pace, letting his body guide him without hurry. There was no destination in mind, only the act of moving—moving through the night, through the quiet world that seemed to hold its breath around him.

The wind brushed his face, warm yet tinged with the coolness of evening. It didn't feel like a rush of air anymore; it felt like a conversation between him and the world. He closed his eyes for a moment, feeling the gentle caress of it on his skin, as though the world itself was reminding him that he was here, that he was alive.

When he opened his eyes, he looked up at the sky. The stars had revealed themselves, a vast, soft canvas of light in the otherwise dark expanse. He had walked this path countless times before, yet tonight, the sky felt endless, stretching far beyond what he could see. The constellations were no longer just distant points of light; they were part of the same breath he was taking, a part of something bigger than himself.

He looked down at his hands for a moment, feeling the smoothness of the stone Mira had given him, still resting gently in his pocket. It was strange—something so small, yet it felt like a key, a reminder that he wasn't carrying the weight of the world anymore. For once, he felt empty in the best way possible. Not hollow, but spacious. He wasn't trying to hold everything together anymore. He wasn't forcing anything. He was simply... being.

His footsteps were in rhythm with the night, a quiet pulse beneath the silence. There were no thoughts spinning in his head, no judgments about where he was or where he was going. It was just him, the night, and the breath of the world moving through him. He couldn't remember the last time he had felt so... unburdened. So present.

When he arrived at his apartment, he stood outside for a moment, the door just a few feet away, before stepping inside. The place felt different now—less like a refuge from life and more like a space where life could happen. He tossed his keys on the table, letting them fall where they may. The mess that Mira had encouraged him to embrace wasn't an inconvenience anymore. It was just... life. His life. In all its messy, imperfect beauty.

He sat at his desk, the journal still waiting. The pages seemed to call to him, each one a reminder of what had shifted in him. With a quiet exhale, he opened it, his pen hovering over the blank page. He thought for a moment, then wrote:

"I thought surrender was defeat. But it's the first time I've truly felt free."

The words flowed easily, almost as if they had always been waiting to be written. For the first time, there was no hesitation. No resistance. He simply wrote what was true.

He set the pen down and closed the journal, letting the night settle around him. For the first time in as long as he could remember, Noah felt the stillness within him—peace, not as something to achieve, but as something he could inhabit.

And for the first time, he knew: surrender wasn't the end. It was the beginning.

PART 6: THE GARDEN OF TRUTH

An Invitation – "A Place Where People Speak the Truth"
Noah awoke to the scent of soft rain and the hush of a world not yet in motion.

It was morning, but not like any other. The kind of morning that didn't demand. It simply arrived, quietly, like a friend you trust enough to sit with in silence. His body felt heavier in the most peaceful way, as if it had been carrying a weight for years and had finally set it down somewhere safe.

His apartment was still messy. Dishes in the sink. Clothes draped across a chair. But for the first time in a long while, he saw it not as disarray—but as evidence of living. The chaos no longer felt like failure. It felt like truth.

On the coffee table, the journal waited.

Its cover worn now, fingerprints etched into the edges. It felt more like a companion than an object. He reached for it instinctively, flipping it open to where he'd left off, but a small white envelope fell from between the pages.

There was no address. No postage stamp. Just his name, written in soft, deliberate script.

Inside was a single card. No sender. No logo. Just a sentence, hand-penned in black ink:

"You're ready for Eden. Come spend a weekend where people speak the truth."

Noah stared at the words for a long time. A weekend? With who? Where? How did they even know—

He stopped himself. That old spiral of needing to figure it all out before taking a step. The same spiral that had kept him from most of his life.

But this wasn't a demand. It was an invitation.

His fingers traced the ink again. "Where people speak the truth."

His heart fluttered. Not in fear, but in recognition.

He stood, slowly, almost reverently, and looked around his apartment—the evidence of his undoing still visible. But now it was paired with something new: the beginning of his becoming.

Noah packed a small bag. Not carefully. Not with obsessive lists or folded shirts arranged by color. Just enough for the weekend. Clothes he felt like himself in. The journal. The stone from Mira. And a willingness to see what was next.

The train station was unusually quiet for a Friday.

As the train pulled away from the city, he let his body relax into the rhythm of movement. The city shrank behind him, its noise fading into the distance. Rain streaked softly across the window, and with it came an unexpected sense of reverence. He wasn't running away. He was moving toward something—for the first time without knowing exactly what.

He opened the journal and turned back through its pages. His own handwriting met him:

"I thought surrender was defeat. But it's the first time I've truly felt free."

The words grounded him.

Halfway through the journey, the landscape began to change. The buildings gave way to fields. The roads became narrower. Trees arched over the tracks like gentle sentinels. Noah leaned his forehead against the cool windowpane and closed his eyes.

He felt like he was on a pilgrimage. Not religious, not traditional—but sacred nonetheless. A journey back to himself, to truths he hadn't yet spoken, to feelings he'd buried too deeply to name.

A small sign at a country stop greeted him when he stepped off the train.

"Eden."

There was no fanfare. No one holding a sign. Just a winding path that led into the woods, and a sense that he was exactly where he was supposed to be.

He followed it.

Birdsong accompanied him. So did the scent of pine and rain-soaked earth. His steps slowed naturally, as if the land itself was inviting him to walk with care, to listen with more than ears.

Eventually, the path opened.

There it was.

A sprawling garden, wild yet deliberate. Flowers of every color, trees that whispered in the breeze, wooden structures that looked built by hand—low cabins nestled in greenery, hammocks strung between trees, and a large open-air pavilion that smelled of jasmine and cedarwood.

It didn't look like a retreat center. It looked like someone had dreamed of peace and planted it.

In the center stood a woman.

She wasn't striking in the way magazines define beauty. But something about her presence made Noah stop. She had silver-streaked hair pulled back into a loose braid and eyes that held the kind of softness people rarely earn. She wasn't trying to be anything. She just *was*.

She smiled when she saw him.

"Noah," she said, like she already knew him.

He felt his throat tighten slightly. "You're Eden?"

She shook her head gently. "No. Eden isn't a person. It's a space. A way of being."

He nodded slowly, unsure what to say. But the way she spoke soothed something in him.

"I'm just the gardener," she said with a wink, then turned and walked toward the garden path. "Come. Your bed is ready. So is your truth."

That night, in a cabin lit only by lanterns and fireflies, Noah lay awake listening to the wind rustle through the trees outside. There was no cell signal. No wifi. Just the soft hum of the earth and his own breath.

He didn't feel anxious.

He felt... open.

As he lay on the simple bed beneath a cotton blanket, the words from the journal echoed again:

"There is more wisdom in your breath than in your mind."

He placed one hand over his chest.

And breathed.

Not to get anywhere. Not to fix anything.

Just to feel the life inside him.

Something was blooming.

And it was beginning with truth.

Arriving at the Retreat – The Garden as Metaphor

Noah followed the narrow path as it curled like a quiet ribbon through a forest of tall pines and sun-dappled oaks. The city was far behind him now—its sirens and schedules, its pressure and pretense—and in its place was birdsong, breeze, and the sound of his own footsteps over soft, damp earth.

The air changed here. It wasn't just cleaner—it was *alive*. Scented with rosemary, wild mint, and the deep hum of moss-covered soil. Every breath he took felt like an unspoken permission: to slow down, to soften, to stay.

Then, just as the trail rounded a gentle bend, the trees opened—and there it was.

The garden.

A vast, radiant clearing nestled between wooded hills, ringed with wildflowers and untamed hedges. Pathways of stone wound through knee-high grass and clusters of lavender. Bees drifted lazily between blooms, and sunlight danced like liquid gold through the branches above.

In the center stood a modest lodge—weathered wood, wide windows, and an open porch wrapped in vines. Around it, scattered with no rigid symmetry, were wooden cabins half-covered in ivy and moss. A hammock swayed between two olive trees. Someone laughed gently in the distance. Somewhere, wind chimes whispered their approval.

It didn't feel like a retreat.

It felt like something ancient had grown itself here. Like nature had made a pact with humanity to build a space where truth could breathe.

Noah paused at the edge of it all, struck dumb by the beauty. But more than that—by the feeling. It was as if the land itself had been waiting for him. Not with impatience, but with deep knowing.

He walked forward slowly, taking it in.

A woman stood in the garden ahead, barefoot on the sun-warmed stone path. Her hair was loosely pinned, streaked with silver like twilight, and her linen dress billowed just slightly in the breeze. She was kneeling near a patch of calendula, her hands gently cradling the stem of a blossom as if in silent prayer. When she looked up, her smile wasn't one of welcome—it was one of *recognition*.

She didn't ask his name. Didn't greet him with politeness.

She just stood.

Met his gaze.

And nodded.

There was no need for introductions. She saw him, and he knew it.

Her eyes were deep wells of kindness—yes—but not the gentle kind that pities or tiptoes. This was the kindness that holds you accountable to who you truly are.

She walked toward him without hurry, her feet bare against the earth. When she reached him, she placed her hand over her heart and spoke in a voice that felt like water finding its own level.

"Here," she said, "we don't fix. We *feel*. And what we feel, we *free*."

The words landed in Noah's chest like warm rain after drought.

She turned, as if that was all he needed to know for now, and motioned gently for him to follow.

As they walked the winding path deeper into the garden, past a row of fig trees and a circular bench made from fallen cedar, Noah felt something strange happening inside him.

He wasn't gripping.

He wasn't bracing.

He was... arriving.

Every corner of this place whispered an invitation—not to change, not to prove, but to remember.

Remember softness.

Remember stillness.

Remember the self he'd hidden beneath years of striving and self-containment.

They passed a young man sitting cross-legged in a patch of clover, eyes closed, face lifted to the sun. A couple resting together in a quiet alcove, hands intertwined, not speaking. A woman hanging herbs to dry beneath a shaded awning. Each one offered a glance or a nod, but no one imposed. No one performed.

There was no small talk.

Only presence.

Noah was led to a small wooden cabin tucked beneath the arms of an old elm tree. Its door was ajar. Inside: a simple bed, a shelf with a candle and an old ceramic mug, a window facing the sunrise. No television. No distractions. Just what was needed—and nothing more.

Before leaving, Eden turned to him one last time.

She touched her own chest lightly and said, "This place will show you what you're still holding. But it will also remind you of what's always been yours."

Then, without ceremony, she walked away—her bare feet whispering over stone and soil.

Noah stood in the doorway for a long moment.

And then he stepped inside, not into a room—but into the quietest, most intimate part of himself.

It didn't feel like arrival.

It felt like home.

The First Circle – The Practice of Truth Speaking

The sun had just begun to set, casting long amber shadows across the garden paths. The air carried the faint scent of chamomile and woodsmoke. Somewhere in the distance, a wind chime offered a single soft note, then stilled, as if even sound had paused to listen.

Eden stood beneath a wide oak tree, lantern in hand. One by one, the guests emerged from their cabins and drifted toward her, drawn like quiet moths toward flame. Noah followed the soft trail of light, his footsteps muffled by the grass, heart thudding in anticipation.

They gathered in a wide circular clearing in the heart of the garden. Lanterns hung low in the trees, their glow warm and golden. Cushions and woven mats formed a wide circle on the earth. In the center: nothing but a single unlit candle on a smooth stone, waiting.

Noah sat cross-legged on a cushion, his spine tight, palms flat on his thighs. The others sat around him—twelve in all. Strangers, and yet not. No names had been exchanged. No stories shared. And still, there was an intimacy here that unsettled and calmed him in equal measure.

Eden stood for a moment, letting the silence settle.

Then, she knelt and lit the center candle with a single match.

Its flame flickered, catching and steadying, and when she spoke, her voice was a thread woven through the quiet.

"This is the first circle," she said. "A space where truth is not judged, corrected, or fixed. It is simply spoken."

She looked at each of them with that steady, grounding gaze.

"One by one," she continued, "you'll speak a truth you've never said aloud. It doesn't have to be dramatic. Just *real*. Something your body has been carrying. Something that hasn't been witnessed—until now."

Noah felt his mouth go dry. His hands were already beginning to sweat.

"There will be no response. No advice. No applause. Just presence. Just the truth, rising."

And then she folded her hands in her lap and went still.

The silence stretched long enough to be uncomfortable. Then longer still, until it wasn't. Until it began to feel like something sacred.

A woman across the circle exhaled shakily and spoke first.

"I've been pretending to be okay for over twenty years."

Silence.

A man near the edge said, "I don't love the person I became to survive my childhood."

Silence.

Another voice, softer than the wind: "I don't know how to be touched without flinching."

Each confession rose and fell like breath.

Noah felt them land in his body—each one like a pebble tossed into a still lake, sending ripples inward.

And then, too soon, the circle turned to him.

He hadn't prepared. Hadn't chosen a truth. His throat tightened. A thousand phrases rushed forward, then fell apart.

He looked around the circle.

No one stared. No one waited with expectation. They simply held space, quietly, fully. Like a forest listening.

Noah swallowed.

His voice, when it came, was quieter than he meant. But it was real.

"I never learned how to need people," he said, "without feeling weak."

There it was.

He didn't look up. His gaze stayed fixed on his hands, which now trembled against his knees.

The silence that followed was deep—not empty, but full.

Full of understanding.

Of shared recognition.

Of space that neither clung nor corrected.

No one rushed to reassure him.

No one filled the quiet.

And for the first time in his life, Noah didn't shrink inside his own truth. He didn't need to wrap it in logic or soften it with humor.

He had spoken.

And he was still here.

Whole.

Breathing.

Free.

A heat rose behind his eyes—not shame, not even sadness, but release. His chest softened, his jaw loosened. Something ancient let go inside him.

Truth, it seemed, didn't need to be loud.

It just needed to be allowed.

As the circle continued, Noah sat still, the candle flickering before him, the warmth of the earth beneath him, and a strange, unfamiliar sensation opening gently in his chest.

It was something like... peace.

Time with Eden – Honesty as Softness, Not Shame

The morning sun filtered gently through the trees, laying golden lace across the garden paths. Dew still clung to the edges of the petals, and birdsong filled the space between each breath. Noah walked beside

Eden, the two of them meandering slowly through rows of herbs, wildflowers, and tomato vines heavy with fruit.

Eden moved with a quiet reverence, touching each plant as though greeting an old friend. She wore no shoes. Her feet were stained with earth. A straw basket hung from one arm, half-filled with lavender and lemon balm.

Noah watched her for a moment before breaking the silence. "You know this place like it's a person."

Eden smiled without looking up. "It *is* a person, in a way. Everything that lives responds to how it's seen. Tended. Spoken to."

She stopped at a small bush of mint, kneeling to pinch away a few dead stems. "A plant only thrives when you stop yelling at it for not blooming."

Noah chuckled softly. "That's... poetic. And a little on the nose."

She glanced up, eyes playful. "Maybe. Or maybe it's just true."

They kept walking. The gravel crunched softly beneath their steps.

"You were brave last night," Eden said eventually. "Not just for speaking—but for staying with what you said."

Noah looked down at the path. "I've said things before. In therapy. To friends. But I always felt like I had to defend it. Explain it. Apologize for it."

He paused. "Last night was different. I said it, and no one tried to fix it."

"That's the difference between honesty and confession," Eden said, plucking a sprig of rosemary. "Confession says, *I'm wrong, help me be better.* Honesty says, *This is what's real. Please see me anyway.*"

They turned a corner where a willow tree arched low over a stone bench. Eden sat and gestured for him to join her. The garden around them buzzed with soft life—bees, distant wind chimes, the hum of things unspoken but deeply felt.

Noah hesitated. His chest was tight again. Something wanted to rise.

"I've always tried to be the strong one," he said finally. "Reliable. In control. Put-together. But it was never really strength. It was just... keeping everything inside where no one could judge it."

Eden didn't respond. She just looked at him, fully present.

Noah's voice dropped. "There's something I've never said to anyone. Not really."

He swallowed.

"I hurt someone once. Years ago. I didn't cheat or lie or anything dramatic. I just... shut down. She needed more from me, emotionally, and I couldn't give it. I didn't even try. I convinced myself it was her problem. That she was 'too much.' But she wasn't. I just couldn't handle being needed. I left, and I told myself I did the right thing. But I think I was just scared."

The words fell out like stones.

"I've carried that shame for years. That I failed someone who cared about me. And that maybe I'll always do that. Maybe I don't know how to love anyone fully—not even myself."

Silence.

And then Eden said, gently, "What if your shame isn't asking to be solved—but to be seen?"

Noah blinked.

"I don't know how to do that," he admitted. "I've spent so long judging myself for it."

"Then try something else," Eden said. "Try loving the part of you that shut down. The version of you who didn't know how to stay. He wasn't trying to hurt anyone. He was trying to survive."

Noah looked at her, eyes glassy. "Why does that make me want to cry?"

Eden smiled. "Because it's not shame. It's tenderness."

A bird flitted nearby. A breeze moved the leaves. And in the quiet, Noah felt something subtle shift—not a sudden healing, but a loosening. A breath inside a wound. The beginning of mercy.

For once, he didn't rush to explain or make it go away.

He just sat there, beside Eden, feeling his truth held—not as a burden, but as part of him.

And for the first time, that part felt like it might be worthy of love too.

The Reflection Ritual – Writing in the Garden

The afternoon sun had mellowed into a honeyed glow, spilling soft warmth across the meadows and winding paths of the retreat. Eden stood in the center of the garden circle, barefoot as always, her voice low and reverent as she addressed the small group gathered around her.

"In this ritual," she said, "we let the garden hold our truths."

She held up a smooth stone, the size of her palm. Etched into it—hand-carved and weather-worn—was a simple question: *What truth inside you still asks to be welcomed?*

Around her, an assortment of similar stones were laid out in a basket, each one bearing the same prompt.

"Take one," she said. "Then find a quiet place. Let your truth meet the earth. Let your heart speak."

Noah stepped forward with the others, picking a stone that felt warm in his hand, as if it had been waiting for him. A volunteer handed him a small linen-bound journal and a pen tied with twine. He wandered down a shaded path until he came to a quiet alcove between two olive trees, where sunlight dappled the ground and a wooden bench invited him to sit.

Birdsong filled the space. The scent of basil and crushed petals hung on the breeze. The world felt hushed—listening, waiting.

Noah opened the journal, set the stone on the bench beside him, and stared at the blank page for a long moment. Then, slowly, the words began to spill.

What truth inside me still asks to be welcomed?

The truth that I've built my life on scaffolding—carefully constructed personas, curated strength, silence in all the places I should have screamed.

The truth that I thought being composed meant being worthy.

That vulnerability was a costume I wore only when it could be controlled.

That I became so good at pretending I didn't need comfort, I forgot what comfort felt like.

That I've mourned things without allowing myself to grieve—dreams I buried, words I never said, love I let slip through my fingers because I was too afraid to be fully seen.

That beneath every mask, there is still a boy who wanted to be enough just as he was.

That my need to be needed swallowed my ability to need.

That I carry shame not because I'm broken—but because no one ever told me it was okay to bloom slowly.

He paused, letting the ink dry, the wind brushing against his cheek like a gentle acknowledgment. A leaf drifted down beside him, spiraling softly before resting on the ground.

He breathed in deeply—earth, sun, breath, sky—and then wrote:

I am not broken. I'm just blooming in slow motion.

A stillness came over him. Not the rigid kind he used to confuse with control, but a soft spaciousness. A feeling of being exactly where he needed to be. Of being exactly *who* he needed to be.

He looked at the stone once more, its question now answered with quiet grace.

Somewhere nearby, Eden's wind chime sang in the breeze.

And Noah closed the journal, not to shut it—but to let the truth inside it echo gently, unashamed, in the garden of his becoming.

Leaving Eden – Carrying the Garden Within

The morning of departure was silver-soft, wrapped in dew and hush. Mist lingered just above the garden's edges, like the retreat itself didn't want to let go. Birds called gently to one another, and the trees stood in still ceremony as Noah walked slowly through the worn stone path toward the garden's heart one last time.

Eden was there, kneeling beside a cluster of lavender, her fingers brushing the stems with affection, as though saying goodbye to them, too. When she saw Noah, she rose gracefully, dusting her palms on her linen skirt.

They didn't speak at first. The silence between them had become familiar, even sacred.

Finally, Eden held something out to him—a small, square envelope wrapped in thin twine. Inside, he found a single pressed calendula flower, its golden-orange petals perfectly preserved, and a tiny folded page torn from what looked like a journal.

Her handwriting curved across the paper with quiet care:

"The truth isn't a destination. It's a companion. Let it walk with you."

She placed a hand gently over his, holding the note and flower between them.

"This is yours now," she said softly. "Not just this—this space you found. But the way you held yourself while you found it."

Noah didn't know how to respond. Not in words. So instead, he stepped forward and wrapped his arms around her—not fluidly, not smoothly. His movements were hesitant, unfamiliar, but real.

Eden smiled against his shoulder, returning the hug without hesitation.

When they pulled apart, her eyes shimmered—not with tears, but with something deeper. Something like pride. Something like seeing a seed take root.

Noah made his way toward the gate, his pack light on his shoulder, his steps unhurried. With each stride, he noticed how differently he moved—his spine less braced, his jaw unclenched, his breath softer, fuller. He didn't walk like someone fleeing. He walked like someone arriving, even as he left.

As the retreat faded into the rearview of memory, he carried no panic, no need to "hold on." The garden, he realized, was not behind him.

It had taken root in him.

Back home, the evening was quiet. He opened the Law of Release journal and sat beside the window, the envelope resting nearby. The calendula lay on the open page, vibrant even in stillness.

He picked up his pen, and without hesitation, wrote:

"Honesty is not a weapon. It is a window. And when I opened it, the wind smelled like peace."

He closed the journal with a steady hand. No finality in the gesture—just a pause.

Outside, the night was warm. A breeze moved through the open window, brushing his cheek with the same gentle hush he remembered from Eden's garden.

And for the first time in his life, Noah didn't brace himself against the future.

He simply let it in.

PART 7: SHADOWS IN THE LIGHT

The Phone Call – The Past Knocks Loudly

The suitcase sat half-unzipped on the bedroom floor, spilling soft, earthy-smelling clothes onto the rug. Noah stood beside it barefoot, hands resting lightly on the frame of the window. Late afternoon sunlight painted golden squares on the wooden floor, and the peace of Eden still lingered in the room like a scent—faint, but unmistakable.

He felt different. Still. Open. The kind of calm that doesn't beg to be noticed but settles in the bones.

His journal rested on the nightstand, and earlier that morning he had written:

"I trust the quiet now. I no longer rush to fill it."

But the quiet, as it turned out, had other plans.

His phone buzzed once.

Then again.

He walked over casually, expecting a message from Julian, maybe Mira. But when he picked it up, the screen stopped him cold.

Dad.

No image. Just the name. Unchanged since the last time it had appeared—four years ago, maybe five. Long enough for the name to become a ghost.

Noah stared. He didn't touch it. He didn't breathe.

Then came the voicemail notification.

His thumb hovered. He considered ignoring it—just pressing delete and moving on. He had every reason to. The man had vanished from his life with more silence than storm, leaving Noah to carry answers he'd never received.

But something pulsed in his chest. Not urgency. Not pain. Something older. A weight unacknowledged.

He tapped play.

"Hey. It's me."

The voice was rough, aged in a way Noah didn't remember.

"Your uncle passed. Thought you should know." A pause. *"I'm around if you want to talk."*

Click.

That was it.

Noah sat down slowly on the edge of the bed, the phone still in his hand. The sun shifted across the floor like time had just leapt without warning. The air in the room thickened.

Across from him, the journal sat open to the last page he had written before leaving Eden. His own handwriting stared back:

"The truth you avoid is the one that holds your freedom."

His jaw clenched. His breath caught at the top of his lungs and refused to move.

Why now? After all this time—after he had finally begun to feel whole?

He stood abruptly and began pacing. Memories stirred uninvited: a slammed door, a disappointed glare, the endless stretch of teenage silence between them. His father hadn't known how to comfort. Only how to correct. Their last conversation had ended in cold logic, not emotion. Noah had left thinking it was over.

And yet.

His father's voice in that message hadn't sounded cold. It hadn't sounded cruel. It had sounded... tired.

Fragile.

That's what scared him most.

Because the moment you stop hating someone is the moment you realize you're not protected from them anymore.

Noah sat back down and placed the phone next to the journal. His hands trembled slightly.

He whispered aloud, like testing the shape of a thought:

"What if I'm ready... but still afraid?"

The quiet answered, as it always had. Not with words, but with space.

He picked up the pen. Wrote slowly, deliberately:

"I don't know what I want from him. Maybe nothing. Maybe closure. But if I've learned anything, it's this: the parts of me I silence don't disappear—they wait. And sometimes, they knock."

He stared at the phone again.

It didn't buzz this time.

But it might as well have.

Because the past was no longer content being locked away. It had knocked gently, yes.

But now it waited—for the door to open.

The Memories Return – Old Wounds in a New Light

The evening settled in like smoke—slow, creeping, nearly invisible until it filled the room.

Noah sat on the floor, knees pulled to his chest, leaning against the wall in his apartment. The lamp beside him cast soft amber light across the room, brushing gently over half-packed bags and a coffee mug gone cold. His phone lay face down on the windowsill. He hadn't touched it since the voicemail.

Outside, the city moved on, unaware. Horns in the distance. A siren somewhere too far to matter. The hum of life continuing. But inside, Noah was quiet. Not calm—quiet, like the air before a storm breaks open.

His thoughts circled in loops, memories threading in through the silence like ghosts returning home.

He was twelve. Rain pelted the windows of their small suburban home. He had gotten second place in a local piano competition, and he'd come home clutching the certificate like a fragile treasure.

He remembered the way he'd looked up at his father, eyes wide, hope high in his throat.

"I played my best," he'd said.

His father hadn't looked up from his desk. "Second place isn't best. It's almost best."

A pause. Then, quieter: "Next time, focus more."

Noah had nodded like that made sense. Like it didn't crack something in him.

He could still feel the weight of the certificate in his hand, the way it seemed to dull in color the moment his father spoke. The memory wasn't new—it had played in his mind like a worn-out tape for years. But something about it felt... different now.

He could still feel the ache. But it wasn't burning anymore. It was duller, rounder. Like grief softened by time.

He sighed, rubbing his palm over his chest. Then, another memory surfaced—one he hadn't thought of in years.

Seventeen. In the garage. Noah had just finished writing a song—one of his earliest—and he'd found the courage to play it. His father stood at the workbench, fiddling with something in his hands.

Noah had barely finished the last chord when his father said, "Is that what you want to do with your life? Play sad songs in a garage?"

Noah had laughed it off, but he remembered how the laughter stuck in his throat.

Now, sitting on the floor with the hum of the lamp in his ear, Noah whispered to the empty room, "What if he did the best he could... and it still wasn't enough?"

He closed his eyes. That sentence hung in the air like incense smoke. Not quite forgiveness. Not a pass.

Just... space.

He'd spent years trying to be louder than that silence, sharper than that disappointment. Trying to outgrow the boy who never felt good enough. But now, he saw something new: the man his father might've been. A man raised by someone even colder. A man with his own silences and bruises he never named.

Noah opened his eyes. They didn't sting like they used to. The memories still ached—but they no longer ruled him. He didn't flinch.

That felt new.

He leaned his head back against the wall and let out a long, slow breath. Maybe it wasn't about making peace with the past, not yet. Maybe it was just about telling the truth about it.

And the truth was: he still carried the ache.

But it didn't carry him anymore.

The Confrontation – A Dinner Table of Unspoken Things

The diner was nothing special. A faded sign outside blinked softly—*Daisy's Diner*, and the neon light flickered like a tired breath. The booths were worn, the air thick with the smell of coffee and greasy food. The place had an aura of familiarity that felt like the past itself—just enough warmth to keep the chill at bay.

Noah sat in the corner booth, stirring his coffee absentmindedly. He'd been there for ten minutes, waiting. His father was late, as usual. But today, Noah didn't mind the waiting. He felt a strange sense of stillness, like he'd already crossed a line without knowing it.

When the bell above the door jingled, Noah didn't need to look up to know it was his father. The shuffle of heavy boots on the floor. The slight creak of a chair as his father lowered himself into the booth across from him. The familiar scent of aftershave and the faint whiff of tobacco.

He looked older—grayer, a little frailer. The hardness in his face had softened, but it hadn't disappeared. There was still that line of tension in his jaw, like everything was a battle he wasn't sure he wanted to fight anymore.

"Long time," his father said, the words flat, no warmth.

Noah met his gaze, but only for a second before looking back down at his coffee. The silence stretched between them, heavy and awkward.

"How's work?" Noah asked, his voice sounding too polite, too careful.

"Same as always," his father replied, almost absent. "Still fixing things. Keeping busy."

Another pause.

Noah felt the wall building between them, like always. His father was already shutting down, deflecting. He wasn't ready for anything deeper. But Noah couldn't let it slide this time. The ache was still too raw, too present.

He put the coffee cup down slowly, his fingers lingering on the edge. His mind was a thousand miles away, thinking of everything he'd been carrying all these years. The questions he'd never asked. The silence that had built his entire childhood.

"Dad," Noah said, his voice low but firm. "Did you ever wonder how it felt to never be enough for you?"

His father's eyes flickered, just for a second, before he looked away. The breath he let out was sharp, defensive. He shifted in his seat, trying to find a way to evade it, but Noah wouldn't let him.

"Noah, don't do this," his father muttered, like the words were something he couldn't quite face.

"I'm not doing anything. I'm asking. You've never answered, and I'm wondering if you even know." Noah felt his pulse quicken. His voice was getting steadier, sharper. The tension in the room was rising, but it wasn't angry. It was just... raw.

"Maybe you don't understand," his father muttered, looking away toward the window. His voice was small, almost fragile. "I did the best I could. I didn't know how to—"

"No, you didn't," Noah interrupted, his heart pounding. "You didn't know how to what? Love me? To show me you cared? You were always so busy trying to make me *something*—something I never was. I tried so hard to be what you wanted, and you never even looked. You never saw me. You only saw the damn idea of who I should be."

There it was. The words he'd swallowed for years. The anger he'd bottled up. The disappointment that had festered until it could no longer stay hidden.

His father flinched, his face tightening. For a moment, there was nothing but the quiet of the diner, the clink of a spoon somewhere behind them, and the sound of Noah's breath filling the space between them.

"I *tried*," his father said again, more desperate now. He was looking at Noah like he didn't understand this version of him, like he was lost in a memory he couldn't reach. "I didn't know how to do any of this. I was trying to keep you safe. Trying to give you everything I didn't have."

Noah's chest tightened, the old hurt churning, but there was something else, too—something unfamiliar. The anger had softened into something gentler. He leaned back, looking at his father, who seemed so much smaller now, like the man who had once cast such a long shadow had somehow lost his power.

"I know," Noah whispered, his voice breaking slightly. "I know you did. But you *didn't* give me what I needed. You didn't teach me how to be me. How to be vulnerable, how to just exist without having to prove everything all the time."

His father's hand trembled slightly on the table, and for the first time, Noah saw him not as a distant figure, but as a man—flawed, afraid, maybe even broken in his own way.

"You're right," his father said, his voice finally cracking. "I'm sorry. I didn't know how to love you the way you needed."

It wasn't much. It wasn't a complete apology. But it was something.

Noah nodded, slowly. His chest felt lighter, somehow, but there was no sense of resolution. Not yet. But maybe there didn't need to be. Maybe the only thing that mattered was the truth, finally spoken.

The silence between them now wasn't suffocating. It was different. The tension was still there, but it was softer, less heavy. It was a quiet understanding. A moment of raw honesty.

Noah sat back, looking at his father—not with anger, not with bitterness, but with something new. A willingness to see him, even if he could never fully understand him.

They sat there for a while, the diner's quiet hum around them, two men who had never really known each other, but who, for a moment, had tried to. And in that effort, something had cracked.

The Collapse – Aftermath and Emotional Fallout

The night air was sharp against Noah's skin as he walked, his footsteps echoing in the empty streets. The diner was a distant memory now, fading with every step he took away from it. His hands were stuffed deep into his pockets, but no matter how hard he tried, he couldn't seem to warm up.

He felt raw—torn open in a way he hadn't anticipated. The words with his father had left him drained, hollowed out. The ache in his chest wasn't from anger or resentment anymore; it was something deeper, something unfamiliar. It was grief—a slow, pulsing grief that he couldn't run from.

With every breath, he felt it. The vulnerability. The exposure. His chest was tight, constricted, as if he were holding onto something that didn't belong to him anymore. His mind replayed fragments of the conversation—the tremor in his father's voice, the weight of his own words, the silence that followed. None of it felt resolved. Nothing had shifted in the way he'd expected. They hadn't fixed anything.

But still, the sting of it all lingered.

The streets were nearly empty now, the city noises dimming to a low hum. The cool night brushed against his face, but it did nothing to ease the chaos in his mind. His father's face—older, worn, regretful—kept flashing before his eyes. The words that had slipped out, the ones he couldn't take back. He wasn't sure whether to regret them or to embrace them.

Why did it hurt so much? Why couldn't he feel any peace, even though he knew he'd done the right thing?

Part of him wanted to scream—to demand that it all make sense. But another part of him just... walked. He kept moving, even though he didn't know where he was going. His body wanted to run away from everything, from the conversation, from his father, from the overwhelming swell of emotions he couldn't process fast enough. But his feet kept carrying him, step after step, as if the act of walking alone would somehow heal him.

When he finally arrived back at his apartment, it felt too quiet—too still. The city's noise had vanished, leaving only the silence that pressed against his skin like a weight. He opened the door, the familiar scent of his living room greeting him. The walls felt cold, like they were watching him. Waiting. The journal sat on the coffee table, as if it had been patiently waiting for him to come back.

He walked over to it, each step feeling heavier than the last. The weight of the night pressed on him like an anchor, pulling him into the depths of his own thoughts. He sat down, staring at the journal for a moment, his fingers trembling as he reached for it.

The words came slowly, but they came.

"I let him speak. I let myself speak. We didn't fix anything. But maybe that's not the point."

The pen shook in his hand as he wrote, the words spilling out in jagged sentences. He wasn't sure what he was trying to say—only that he needed to write it down. He needed to give it shape, to make it real.

"I wanted it to be fixed. I wanted the pain to stop. But maybe there's no 'fixing' this. Maybe there's just... recognition. Recognition that the hurt is still there. That it's always been there. And that's okay."

Noah paused for a moment, staring at the words. He wasn't sure if he believed it, but something in him wanted to. Wanted to believe that just acknowledging the pain could somehow make it easier to carry.

He wasn't sure how to make sense of the conversation, of what had transpired between him and his father. Nothing had been solved. No apologies had been fully given. But the air between them had shifted. And in some strange way, that had to be enough.

Sometimes, Noah thought, the release wasn't about resolving everything. It wasn't about finding closure or making peace. Sometimes, the release was simply about *feeling* it—about *letting* it be. Letting the pain exist, without trying to erase it.

Maybe the truth wasn't always something that could be fixed. Maybe the truth was just something you had to *live with*.

"I spoke the truth," he wrote. "And it still hurts. But it feels lighter somehow. Like it's not *just mine* anymore. Maybe that's all I can ask for right now."

The words on the page felt like a sigh, like an exhale after holding something in for too long. The ache in his chest had softened a little, but it still lingered. The pain hadn't disappeared. It wasn't *gone*—but somehow, it didn't feel as suffocating as it had before.

Noah leaned back, running a hand over his face. The room around him felt too quiet, too still. But for the first time in a long while, he didn't feel like he was drowning in it. He felt... *present* in it. Present in the weight of the past. Present in the mess of it all.

And maybe that was the most he could hope for tonight.

He closed the journal slowly, as if it were a fragile thing. He felt empty—but in a way that allowed room for something else. Maybe for healing. Maybe for peace.

For now, he could accept that the process wasn't neat or clean. It wasn't a straight line. It was messy. It was painful. And it was still unfolding.

And that was enough.

Noah sat in the silence, letting the weight of it all settle in his bones. There was no urgency to move. No need to push it away. For once, he didn't need to fix anything. He just needed to be. Just *breathe*. And that felt like a kind of freedom too.

Mira's Return – What Cannot Be Rewritten, Can Be Reclaimed

Noah was sitting on the edge of his bed when Mira appeared at his door, as if she had slipped in from another world altogether. There was no knocking, no warning. Just a gentle presence, as soft as the morning light that crept in through his window.

He didn't stand to greet her. He didn't need to. She had a way of entering without intrusion, like a calm breeze that brushed past every corner of his soul. She looked at him with those knowing eyes, the ones that saw beyond the walls Noah had spent so many years building.

"Hi," he said, his voice hoarse. He felt as though he were holding the fragments of the previous night's conversation together with his hands, trying to keep the pieces from slipping through his fingers.

Mira said nothing, but there was something in the silence that made him want to break. She closed the door behind her and sat down beside him on the bed, her presence neither overwhelming nor dismissive—just... *there*.

He wanted to speak, wanted to spill out all the confusion, the rawness, but he didn't. He didn't need to. Mira didn't need words to know. She simply rested her hand on his, and the contact was like a thread, fragile and steady, connecting him back to something he'd almost forgotten.

After a moment, Mira stood and motioned for him to follow her. She didn't need to ask him twice. He followed her through the quiet apartment, his mind still a flurry of emotions he couldn't sort out. When they reached the small corner by his window, where soft light filtered through the blinds, she gestured to the floor.

"Sit with me," she said, her voice a soothing balm.

Noah sank down, his legs folding beneath him. Mira sat across from him, still, grounded, her posture as if she were part of the earth itself. He mirrored her, and for a long moment, there was just silence between them. The kind that was heavy with unspoken understanding.

Mira took a deep breath, closing her eyes for a moment, and when she spoke, it was with that calm knowingness that settled deep inside him.

"Close your eyes, Noah," she said softly. "Take a deep breath with me."

Noah obeyed, inhaling deeply. The air was cool in his lungs, but it didn't fill him as it should. There was a heaviness inside, a weight he hadn't known how to carry. But Mira's presence was a steady pull, guiding him to something beyond the clutter of his thoughts.

"Now, imagine the version of yourself—the boy you were—standing in front of you." Her voice was soft, yet unwavering. "See him clearly. What does he look like?"

Noah's breath caught in his chest. His eyes fluttered open briefly, but then he closed them again, letting the image take shape. He saw himself—young, maybe seven or eight—standing in the hallway of his childhood home. His shoulders were slumped, his face a mixture of confusion and hurt, as if he knew something was wrong but couldn't quite understand it.

"He's scared," Noah whispered, the words barely leaving his lips.

"Yes," Mira agreed. "He's scared. But he's also brave. He's doing the best he can with what he has."

Noah's chest tightened as the memory of that boy—the one who had tried so hard to win love, to be enough—flooded him. His throat closed with emotion. He had spent so much time running from that child, thinking he had to leave him behind to grow, to be strong. But now he saw that boy clearly. And for the first time, he wanted to hold him. Protect him.

"You've spent so many years trying to silence him," Mira's voice was gentle but firm. "Telling him that his pain wasn't enough, that his needs were too much. But the truth is, Noah—he *deserves* love. He deserves tenderness. And you, now, are the one who can give him that."

Noah shook his head slightly, the tears already beginning to blur his vision. "But I wasn't enough. I could never make him feel enough." The words were jagged, sharp, like stones falling from his mouth.

Mira's gaze softened. She didn't rush to correct him, but her voice was steady. "You were never meant to fix him, Noah. You were meant to hold him. To love him, as you are now. To show him that you're not abandoning him anymore."

Noah's breath shuddered as a sob broke through. The ache, the deep well of it, was there in full force now. He could see that child clearly, could feel the weight of all the unspoken things, the love he hadn't received, the love he hadn't known how to give. He had spent so many years pretending it didn't matter, that it was buried, that he didn't need it.

But he did.

He did need it.

And as he sat there, with Mira's words wrapping around him like a soft embrace, he realized that he wasn't just holding the boy in front of him. He was holding the boy *inside* of him—tender, fragile, in need of care.

"I'm sorry," he whispered, not to Mira, but to that child—*to himself*. The words came through tears, thick and raw. "I'm sorry I let you down."

Mira placed a hand on his heart, not as a way of comforting him, but as a reminder. "You didn't fail him. You couldn't have. But you can love him now. You can reparent him. And in doing so, you reparent yourself."

Her words sank deep, settling like seeds in the soil of his heart.

The flood of emotion continued to pour, but it wasn't the same kind of pain anymore. This wasn't the pain of fighting the past. This was the pain of *acceptance*—the kind that didn't ask for resolution, but for *presence*. For compassion.

Noah felt it then—the release. The deep, aching release. He was no longer fighting to be something he wasn't. He was no longer fighting the parts of him that had once been broken. He was simply *allowing them to be.*

"You can't rewrite your childhood," Mira whispered, "But you can reparent your present. And with each step you take in love, you create a new beginning. For him, and for you."

The tears that had once felt like a storm now felt like rain—washing him clean. The boy was still there, in him, but he was no longer something to fear or to hide. He was a part of Noah—one that deserved love, one that *was* love.

Noah took a deep breath, letting the weight of the words settle. In that moment, he realized that the deeper the shadow, the more powerful the light it hid. And now, that light was beginning to grow—slow, steady, but undeniable.

It was the beginning of something new. Something that couldn't be undone, but could always be reclaimed.

Noah sat at his desk, the journal open in front of him, its pages worn and well-loved. The weight of everything that had unfolded over the past weeks settled in his bones, pressing gently but firmly. He had learned so much—about surrender, about honesty, about pain. And yet, there was a part of him that felt unfinished, like there was one last layer of this story to peel back.

The room was quiet now, the late evening light dimming as he sat alone with his thoughts. His fingers hovered over the page, uncertain. There was still so much to say, but it was different now—there was no rush. He had no more need to prove anything, not to himself, not to anyone. Not even to his father.

He remembered the dinner table. The words that had hung heavy in the air. His father's tired face, his brittle silence, his defenses that Noah had once tried so hard to break through. He thought of how he had wanted to hear his father admit his failures, to feel some sort of closure, some kind of validation. But it hadn't happened. It might never happen.

And that was okay.

The truth had come in pieces, slow and steady. And now, Noah was left with the last part—letting go. Not of his memories or his pain, but of the need for permission. The need for his father's approval. The need for something that would never come.

He picked up the photo that had been resting beside him on the desk, a picture from his childhood. It was one of those old, faded Polaroids—young Noah standing beside his father, his small hand grasping the larger, calloused one. The photo was almost comical, the way they both looked so out of place together—so different. His father's face was hard, a look Noah had always read as indifference. And yet, he knew that boy in the picture had once hoped that one day, the man in it would look at him differently.

But now, looking at the photo, Noah didn't feel the anger or the sadness he once had. Instead, there was just... distance. Not resentment, not relief, but something quieter. Something like acceptance. The boy in the picture was still him, but he no longer needed to carry that picture as a weight.

With steady hands, Noah slid the photo into the journal. It felt like the most natural thing to do—like placing a chapter of his life into its proper place, no longer clinging to it, but acknowledging it.

He reached for the pen and wrote.

"Forgiveness isn't saying it didn't hurt. It's saying I won't be hurt by it anymore."

Noah paused, the pen resting on the page, his thoughts turning over the words. He wasn't erasing his father's shortcomings or his own pain. But he was making a choice. A choice to stop allowing that hurt to shape him, to hold him hostage. He had spent years trying to fix the past, trying to make sense of things that had never made sense. But now, he was letting it go. Not in the way that some stories ask for forgiveness, for closure, for understanding, but in the way that lets him be free *of* it.

He closed the journal gently, pressing it against his chest. It felt different tonight, somehow. The weight wasn't gone, but it had shifted. There was still some hurt there, still some pieces of anger and disappointment. But they no longer had the power to define him.

The garden inside him was growing, even in the shadow. It was slow, but it was there. The seeds had been planted. He wasn't lighter yet, not in the way he had hoped, but he was freer.

Noah stood up and walked to the window. He looked out at the darkened skyline, the streets bathed in the soft glow of streetlights. There was no grand revelation tonight, no sudden shift into peace. Just a quiet knowing that, somehow, he was moving forward. He didn't need to carry the past with him any longer. He could stand on his own.

And that, he realized, was enough.

The journal lay on the desk behind him, the photo nestled within its pages. A small gesture, a quiet release.

But something had changed. It had been subtle, almost imperceptible. But it was there.

The garden inside him was growing. Even in the shadow.

PART 8: THE CHOICE TO FEEL
Echoes of Silence – What Wasn't Said Still Lives Inside

Noah sat in the stillness of his apartment, the hum of the city outside muted by the thick glass of his windows. The room was quiet—too quiet. His mind, however, churned with a constant undercurrent of emotion, things he couldn't quite pin down. It had been days since the confrontation with his father. The aftermath still lingered, the silence between them still reverberating in his chest.

It wasn't that he regretted speaking up—he didn't. But something had been left unsaid, not only to his father, but to himself. He had fought so long to speak his truth, to be heard, to be seen. But in doing so, had he truly allowed himself to feel everything that came with that? Was there more beneath the surface?

He leaned back in his chair, staring at the journal on his desk, the weight of it subtle but ever-present. A strange comfort. It had been his anchor for so long, his place for reflection and release. Tonight, it beckoned to him again. His fingers brushed over the cover, the edges worn smooth from use, and he opened it to find a new line, written in the same familiar hand, though Noah was sure it hadn't been there before:

"Feeling is not weakness. Feeling is witnessing."

Noah read the words again, feeling a stir in his chest. *Feeling is witnessing.* It wasn't a call to fix, or to understand, or even to forgive. It was a call to simply *be*. To allow what had been buried deep within him to rise without judgment or the need to control it.

He closed the journal and leaned back, taking a slow, deliberate breath. What was he afraid of? What had he been running from, all these years? What had he never allowed himself to feel?

He thought about his father's voice—the way it had cracked when he had said, "I'm around if you want to talk." There had been something fragile in it, something so different from the man Noah had known. But Noah hadn't been able to grasp it, not in that moment. His walls had gone up instantly, his default reaction of distance and control. And yet, the vulnerability in his father's voice had left a mark on him. But even more than that, Noah felt the sting of his own unspoken words—the things he had wanted to say but couldn't, or wouldn't, to protect himself from whatever came after.

Tears, he realized, had been close to the surface. But even now, as he sat there, he couldn't seem to let them fall. Instead, he tried to push the feeling down. Not again. *Not now.*

But the words in the journal had a way of finding their mark, piercing through the armor he had worked so hard to build around himself. They weren't calling for action or change—they were calling for acceptance. For stillness. For feeling, without an agenda.

Noah rubbed his face with both hands, the exhaustion from the past few days catching up with him. He had been so caught up in the emotional fallout from his father's visit that he hadn't paused long enough to notice how much pain he was still carrying. Pain from years of unsaid things. Pain from a past that had shaped him but didn't have to define him anymore.

He looked out the window at the darkened city below. It felt like the world outside had moved on, oblivious to the inner storm he was weathering. But Noah knew this was different now. He was no longer running from his emotions, nor could he suppress them. The choice was now clear: feel them or continue to hide, to numb, to distract. But where had that gotten him? How had it served him?

It hadn't. It had only created more space for the silence to grow. Silence in his heart. Silence in his relationships. Silence in his own skin.

"What have I never allowed myself to feel?" he whispered aloud to the empty room.

The question hung there, a soft challenge in the quiet night. And for the first time in a long time, Noah didn't try to push the question away. He let it settle in his chest, let the answer rise on its own.

He had never fully allowed himself to feel the grief. The grief of being unseen. The grief of carrying so much, alone. The grief of being a son who never received the love he craved, but who had spent years pretending he didn't need it. He hadn't let himself mourn the little boy who had tried so hard to earn approval, to be good enough. He hadn't let himself feel how tired he was from carrying the weight of those expectations.

And there was something else, something deeper. Fear. Fear of feeling too much. Fear that if he allowed himself to feel, he might never stop. That the floodgates might open, and the pain might swallow him whole. But that was just a story, he realized. A story that had kept him locked in a small, safe cage of control.

He closed his eyes and took a deep breath, letting it out slowly. The stillness of the room surrounded him, but he didn't feel alone. The choice was his now: to let go of the old ways, to release the fear, and to simply *feel*.

No longer running. No longer hiding.

Slowly, he opened the journal again. This time, he didn't hesitate. He picked up the pen, feeling the weight of it in his hand. The words didn't come in a rush, but they came with truth.

"I've been avoiding my grief," he wrote. "But it's still here, still waiting to be seen."

Noah paused, breathing deeply. He wasn't sure what came next. But he was beginning to realize that sometimes, there was no next. Sometimes, the most important thing was to be right here, in this moment, with the grief, with the tenderness, with the fear, and with the relief that came from finally letting it all in.

He placed the pen down, letting the quiet return to the room. It wasn't a grand breakthrough, but something in him had shifted. A subtle opening. A quiet promise to himself: he would no longer deny what was inside. He would let it breathe.

And in that breath, Noah began to feel the first stirrings of peace.

Mira's Message – "It's Time to Feel it All"

Noah sat at the kitchen table, the late afternoon sun casting a gentle warmth through the window. The apartment was still—quiet in the way that only a place that holds old energy can be. He hadn't heard from his father since their confrontation, but the weight of it lingered in him like a low hum. The silence that had settled after the storm felt almost too loud, too expansive.

He was used to this kind of silence, the silence that came when emotions were tucked away, neatly folded and hidden. But now, it felt different. Uncomfortable.

The journal sat in front of him, its familiar weight reassuring yet slightly foreign. As if it, too, was waiting for him to make a choice. He ran his fingers over the cover, feeling the subtle texture, and opened it. Inside, in Mira's handwriting, was a new line:

"Feeling is not weakness. Feeling is witnessing."

Noah's chest tightened as the words sank in, a gentle stirring in his chest. He had spoken so many truths, but had he really felt them? He had confronted his father, but had he confronted the grief that had been buried for years?

He leaned back in his chair, the weight of his own thoughts pressing down. A part of him wanted to resist, to push away what he felt. He was good at that—he'd spent a lifetime perfecting the art of ignoring emotions that didn't fit neatly into his structured world.

But this was different. He didn't want to keep avoiding. He couldn't.

The doorbell rang, breaking his reverie.

Noah stood slowly, his feet dragging as if the heaviness of his internal world had followed him into the physical space. He opened the door to find a small envelope left on the mat. It was handwritten, the ink slightly smudged in places as if the writer hadn't been worried about perfection.

Inside, a short message from Mira:

"You've been brave in speaking. Now it's time to be brave in feeling."

There was no return address. Just that simple, direct message.

Noah stared at it for a long moment, unsure of what to do next. Then, almost as if guided by an unseen hand, he reached for his jacket and left the apartment.

The walk to Mira's wasn't far, but it felt like a lifetime. With every step, he could feel the tension in his chest slowly release, as if the walk itself was preparing him for whatever came next. When he reached her door, he knocked softly, waiting for a response.

The door opened, and Mira stood there, looking as calm and steady as ever. She didn't say anything at first. Instead, she stepped aside, inviting him in without a word.

Inside, the space was familiar, yet there was something new about it—something more grounded, more intentional. On the small table in the center of the room, there were items carefully placed: a smooth stone, a bowl of water, a burning candle, and a bundle of dried herbs.

Mira gestured to the table. "I've asked you here to begin the next part of your journey. It's time for you to feel what you've been avoiding."

Noah looked at the items. "What am I supposed to do with them?" he asked, his voice more uncertain than usual.

Mira smiled gently. "These are elements—earth, water, fire, and air. Each is connected to a specific emotion. Earth to stability, fire to anger, air to clarity, and water to grief. Choose one."

Noah's eyes lingered on the water, the liquid swirling gently in the bowl. Something about it called to him, though he couldn't explain why.

"I choose water," he said quietly, his voice soft and distant.

Mira nodded, her expression thoughtful. "Then we begin there." She took a seat across from him, her eyes never leaving his.

Noah sat down, the weight of the moment settling over him like a blanket. He wasn't sure what he expected, but he knew that this moment felt different. There was no rushing, no fixing. Just being.

Mira's voice was soft but steady. "Grief is not something to be fixed, Noah. It's something to feel. Allow it to wash over you."

The room grew quiet. The air felt thick with possibility.

And then, without another word, Noah closed his eyes.

The Grief Ritual – A Full-Body Experience

The room felt warmer now, heavier with the stillness that seemed to cling to every corner. Noah sat on the floor, legs crossed, the bowl of water in front of him. Mira was beside him, as steady as ever, a calm presence in the storm he could already feel stirring within himself.

She didn't speak. She simply watched him, her eyes soft and patient, understanding. Her stillness was both comforting and unnerving—like a mirror reflecting what Noah wasn't ready to see, but what he had to.

For the first time since he'd walked in, Noah felt the weight of the room, the air thick and full of expectation. His body was tight, wound up in anticipation, but his mind was still. The journal's message—*Feeling is not weakness. Feeling is witnessing*—echoed in the back of his mind. He hadn't yet fully embraced what that meant.

Mira leaned forward, her voice low. "Close your eyes. And think about everything you've lost. Not just the big losses. The small ones, too. The things you never had a chance to say goodbye to."

Noah hesitated for a moment, but then closed his eyes, his breath shallow. The darkness behind his eyelids felt like a void, a space where memories were waiting to rise, unwelcome but inevitable.

He thought of his father—how distant he'd been, how he'd never been the man Noah had needed him to be. The disconnect, the coldness, had never been enough to shatter him as a child, but it had chipped away at him, piece by piece, until he no longer recognized the boy who had once sought his father's approval.

He thought of the love he had lost, a woman who had slipped through his fingers, the one who had made him believe, for a fleeting moment, that he could be loved without fear. He had let her go too easily, afraid to let her in completely.

And then there was the child he used to be—the one who believed the world was full of possibilities, full of magic. The one who wasn't afraid to feel. That version of him was gone now, buried under years of protecting himself, years of pretending that he was stronger than he truly was.

Tears welled up in Noah's eyes, but they stayed there, trapped behind his eyelids. His chest tightened, the weight of loss pressing down on him, deeper and deeper. His hands clenched into fists, nails digging into his palms as if trying to hold back the flood. His body was tense, locked in a battle with the grief that had been dormant for so long.

Mira's voice cut through the silence. "Let it in, Noah. Feel it. Everything you've buried. It's all still inside of you."

The words broke something open inside of him. The tears didn't stay behind his eyes anymore—they spilled over, running down his cheeks, hot and raw. His breath came in shallow gasps, the ache in his chest growing unbearable, as if he were carrying the weight of the world on his shoulders. He couldn't breathe through it. He couldn't stop it.

He gasped for air, sobbing now, his body shaking violently. The grief didn't come in waves—it slammed into him, relentless and unyielding. It wasn't a quiet sorrow. It was a guttural, primal scream of loss. His chest heaved, and his body trembled with each sob, each broken sound that tore through him. His body felt like it was coming apart, but at the same time, it felt like it was finally coming back together, like something that had been frozen was finally thawing, but it was painful, excruciating.

Mira didn't move. She didn't say anything. She was just there, beside him, her presence a steady, unshakable anchor.

Noah's hands were gripping the floor now, his fingers digging into the carpet like he was trying to hold onto something, anything. But there was nothing to hold. He had to let go. He had to let the grief consume him, let it wash over him, without fighting it. The pain in his chest felt like it was too much, like it would rip him apart, but he didn't stop. He couldn't stop.

His body shook harder now, each sob coming in waves that felt like they might break him. His throat burned, his eyes were swollen, and yet, it was as if his entire being was finally releasing what had been locked inside for years.

He wasn't sure how long it lasted—minutes, hours? Time had lost meaning. All he knew was that the grief was no longer a foreign weight he was carrying. It was a part of him, moving through him. He was allowing it, surrendering to it, no longer fighting it or pretending it wasn't there.

The room was silent except for the sound of his gasping breaths, the quiet sobs that shook his body like waves on a shore. And in that silence, he realized something. It wasn't just the grief that had been suppressed all these years—it was the vulnerability, the softness, the truth of who he had been, and who he had become.

The shaking slowed. The sobs softened. Noah's body was drained, heavy, but there was something else now. A clarity. A realization.

He wasn't broken. He had simply never allowed himself to feel. He had never given himself permission to feel the depth of his pain, to feel the hurt that had shaped him into the man he was now.

The tears stopped, though his chest still ached, still trembled with the remnants of what had just been released. He sat there in the quiet, the world outside still waiting, but he felt different. Lighter, in a way, but not free. Not yet. He was still processing, still unfolding.

Mira didn't speak. She just sat beside him, offering him the space to breathe, to feel. Her presence was all-encompassing, but it wasn't demanding. She didn't need to fix him. She simply needed him to feel.

Noah finally opened his eyes. They were raw, red from crying, but there was something deeper in them now. He wasn't afraid of what he had felt. He wasn't afraid of his grief anymore.

He looked at Mira, his voice shaky but steady. "I was never broken. I was just... unprocessed."

Mira's eyes softened. She nodded gently. "And now, you've begun to process it. This is where the healing starts."

Noah sat there for a long while, the weight of the ritual still sitting in his bones, still pulsing through him. But something inside of him had shifted. The grief wasn't gone. But it wasn't holding him anymore. He was holding it.

And for the first time in a long time, he let himself feel it all.

The Emotional Spectrum – Feeling Beyond Sadness

Noah sat in the quiet of the room, the air still and thick with the residue of grief. His body ached from the release—every muscle felt spent, as though he had just run a marathon with no finish line. His chest was heavy, but lighter than before, the weight of all he had carried not gone but... rearranged. A space had opened within him, and it was still echoing, still humming with the rawness of the ritual.

Mira remained beside him, as steady as always, her presence both soothing and empowering. She didn't speak. She didn't need to. She just let him be, a silent witness to his unfolding.

And then, unexpectedly, something shifted again. A new wave rose from somewhere deep within him—something sharper, more visceral than the quiet ache of grief. It was a crackling heat, rising like steam from a pot left too long on the stove. Anger.

It hit him with a force that made his breath catch in his throat, his chest tightening in a different way. He thought about his father again—how every word between them had always been tinged with disappointment, with a coldness that made Noah feel as if he were never quite enough. The anger surged, hot and jagged, coursing through him like a river at flood stage.

He had never allowed himself to feel this. Not fully. He had always tucked it away, told himself it was pointless, that anger wasn't a luxury he could afford. But now, with the door cracked open, the emotion flowed freely, unchecked.

Noah's hands clenched into fists, his knuckles white. He felt the heat of it in his face, a flush rising to his skin. The air in the room felt different—charged, like a storm was about to break.

"I'm so fucking angry," he muttered under his breath, the words feeling strange coming from his mouth. "Angry at him... angry at me. At the years I wasted pretending I was fine."

Mira's voice was calm, soft. "Good. Let it out. Let the anger move through you. It's not a poison unless you hold it."

Noah's breath came faster, his chest rising and falling with the force of it. But as he let the anger burn, something began to shift. The heat didn't feel dangerous anymore—it felt freeing. It was a release, a way of claiming something that had always been denied to him. For years, he had swallowed his rage, buried it deep beneath layers of self-protection. But now, it was just another emotion, another part of his story.

Slowly, as the anger ebbed, a new feeling replaced it—something lighter. A soft, surprising shift that made Noah exhale, as if he'd been holding his breath for far too long. Laughter. Not just a chuckle, but something deep from within him, a sound of pure joy that bubbled up unexpectedly, like a river breaking through the dam.

It felt like freedom.

He laughed out loud, the sound shaky at first, then building as he thought about Eden's kindness, her gentleness that had cracked him open in ways he hadn't thought possible. He thought of her calm presence, the way she had invited him to feel, without pressure, without expectation. The memory of her walking him through the garden, her hand light on his shoulder as they shared simple words, made him laugh again. She had seen him, truly seen him, before he could see himself. And that was a rare gift.

Mira's smile was small but knowing, a soft invitation to continue.

As the laughter quieted, something new entered the space: peace. It wasn't an epiphany, wasn't a grand revelation. It was simply... stillness. A quiet, steady pulse in the center of him, a calmness that settled deep into his bones. He felt the weight of the world soften, not because it had gone away, but because he had finally begun to feel it all.

He was no longer running from it. The anger, the joy, the sadness, the peace—they were all just weather, moving through him. They didn't define him, didn't control him. They were simply visitors, each carrying their own lesson.

His chest loosened, his hands unclenched. He let out a long breath, feeling the tension dissolve. The air felt fresher, lighter now, and the space inside him didn't feel empty—it felt full, expansive, as if room had been made for everything that had once been shut away.

Mira didn't speak again. She simply sat, watching him with the same quiet understanding, the same calm acceptance. She wasn't there to fix him. She was there to show him how to be with himself, to let him see that every emotion, every sensation, was part of a greater whole.

Noah looked down at the journal, resting on the floor beside him. He picked it up, his fingers tracing the worn edges, the familiar weight of it grounding him. The words in his mind swirled, still fresh from Mira's guidance, still resonating like a bell inside his chest.

He opened the journal and wrote, feeling the words pour out of him without hesitation:

"I am a sky wide enough for every kind of weather."

The mantra felt right. It felt true. He wasn't just a man of grief, or anger, or joy. He wasn't just one thing. He was all of it. The emotions that had once felt like intruders now felt like teachers, each one bringing its own wisdom, its own lesson.

Mira watched him for a moment, her smile softening. "Now you see," she said gently. "When you let yourself feel it all, you become something bigger. You become whole."

Noah closed the journal, a deep sense of peace settling within him. He wasn't fixed. He didn't need to be. He was simply learning to let the emotions flow through him, without resistance. He was learning to be present with them, to honor them, to let them teach him what he needed to know.

For the first time in his life, he felt like he was exactly where he was supposed to be. Not fighting the storms within him, but embracing them, letting them move through him, knowing they would pass. And when they did, he would still be standing, still whole, still learning.

The sky inside him was wide enough for every kind of weather. And for the first time, he was ready to let it all in.

A Letter to Himself – The Ultimate Act of Feeling

The evening was still, the soft hum of the world outside barely reaching Noah's senses. The air in the room felt thick with the weight of everything he had allowed himself to feel in the past days, and yet, there was a new kind of lightness, like the world was breathing with him. He had done the work, felt the pain, tasted the release, and still, the journey was far from over.

Mira sat across from him, a quiet presence, her eyes always soft with understanding. She hadn't said much since the grief ritual, since the emotional spectrum had been allowed to flow freely through him. But now, as they sat in the stillness together, she spoke, her voice gentle yet firm in its invitation.

"I want you to write a letter," she said, her eyes steady on his. "Not to anyone else. Not to your father. Not to your past. But to yourself. The you who resisted. The you who numbed. The you who couldn't feel."

Noah looked at her, a question lingering in his gaze, but she offered nothing but patience.

"Write to him," she said softly, "the part of you that did everything he could just to survive."

He nodded slowly, the weight of her words sinking in. She wasn't asking for perfection. She wasn't asking for something heroic or grand. She was asking him to honor the version of himself that had done what was needed, even if it wasn't always what he wanted. The version of himself that had survived, that had survived without feeling—out of necessity, out of self-protection.

Noah opened the journal, the same familiar pages where his thoughts had poured out time and again. The pen in his hand felt foreign now, yet intimate. He hesitated for a moment, feeling the heavy emotions of the past days swirling inside him, but then he began to write, the words coming slow at first, like a whisper.

Dear Noah,

I know you're tired. I know it's been hard to keep going, to keep pretending that everything was okay when it wasn't. You did what you had to do. You built walls, you numbed, you ran from the things that scared you. And you did it because you didn't know how else to survive. You didn't know how to feel without being overwhelmed by it. And that's okay. You didn't have the tools. You didn't have the space. But you did your best with what you had.

I want you to know I see you. I see the quiet moments where you swallowed the hurt, the rage, the longing. I see how you kept it all inside because you didn't trust that anyone could handle it, that anyone could hold it for you. I see how you learned to hide, to be silent, to keep the pieces of yourself tucked away like they didn't matter.

But I also want you to know that I love you for that. I love you for the silence you chose because it kept you safe. I love you for doing what you needed to do, even if it meant losing parts of yourself along the way. You were doing the best you could, and that's something to honor.

But now... Now, we're ready to feel it all.

We're ready to let the walls come down. We're ready to hear the silence, to feel the sound. The grief, the anger, the joy, the peace—they're all part of us now. And we don't need to run anymore. We don't need to hide anymore. We're ready to open up to what's inside, to what's always been inside.

I know it's scary. I know it feels vulnerable. But we're stronger now. We've made it through the worst, and we're still here. And I love you for that, too. I love you for your resilience, your strength, your tenderness, your silence, and your sound.

So here's to you. To the version of us that survived. To the version of us that's learning to live again. I love you, Noah. All of you.

With everything I have,

Noah

Noah set the pen down, his hand trembling just slightly, as if the weight of the words had finally sunk deep enough into him that his body couldn't quite keep up. His chest felt wide open now, like he had just breathed for the first time in years. The letter wasn't perfect, but it didn't need to be. It was honest. It was real.

He glanced up at Mira, who was still sitting across from him, her eyes calm but alive with a quiet light.

"It's okay to feel everything," she said softly. "It's okay to acknowledge every version of you. You're not losing yourself. You're becoming more of yourself."

Noah nodded, the words settling deep within him. The air felt sacred now, charged with something powerful. He took the letter, folding it carefully, and slid it into the journal. It felt like a final act of release. Not to anyone else. Not for anyone else. Just for him. A moment of grace, a gesture of forgiveness, of acceptance.

Mira stood up, offering him a soft, knowing smile. He wasn't fixed. He wasn't healed. But in that moment, he was whole. He was real. He was beginning to feel it all.

And that was enough.

Noah closed the journal, feeling the weight of the letter inside—his letter to himself, a sacred act of release. As he stood up, a quiet peace settled in his chest, not a calm born from silence, but a peace born from truth.

He was ready to feel it all.

The Quiet Breakthrough – Feeling Without Story

Noah sat on the balcony, the soft evening air brushing his skin, his legs stretched out in front of him. It was quiet. The kind of quiet that settles deep in your bones, where even the city hums a distant lullaby. The sun had long since dipped below the horizon, leaving behind a velvet sky that pulled the day into its stillness. The only sounds were the rustle of leaves, the occasional chirp of a bird, and the rhythmic pulse of his breath.

He had no agenda. No need to fix anything. No deep thoughts swirling or breakthroughs waiting to happen. Just... being.

The journal sat beside him, its pages tucked away with the weight of all the words he had written, the letters he had given to himself. But now, in this moment, there was no need to add anything more. The world around him felt vast, and he felt small—small in the way that feels grounding rather than insignificant.

A tear slipped down his cheek. He didn't know where it had come from, and he didn't need to. It wasn't for anything or anyone. It was just the body's way of feeling, and he let it fall without chasing the reason. His chest felt open, like a door had been left ajar for something to flow out, something that had been contained for far too long.

He closed his eyes, feeling the tear trace its path down his skin, the slight chill of the evening breeze against his damp face. His lips quirked into a smile—subtle, but real. A smile not for anything external, but just because his heart had found its space.

A cloud passed overhead, drifting lazily across the sky, changing shape in the slow rhythm of nature. Noah watched it for a moment, and then he blinked—something shifted within him, just slightly. He realized he didn't need to assign meaning to the cloud, or to the tear, or to the smile. They were just parts of the moment. Parts of being.

He didn't need to figure anything out. Didn't need to understand. Didn't need to keep going in search of something more. The peace he had been chasing wasn't out there, beyond reach, waiting for him to unravel it. It was here. Now. Inside him.

Noah closed his eyes again, letting his thoughts wander off like the cloud, gentle and untethered. There was nothing more to say.

He reached for the journal and opened it to a fresh page. His pen hesitated for a moment, but then it moved, writing with a quiet certainty that felt like a final act of release—simple and complete.

"I always thought I had to understand it to heal it. But maybe I just had to feel it."

Noah set the pen down and closed the journal, letting the words rest there. He didn't need to read them over. He didn't need to go back and analyze. He had felt it. And that, in itself, was enough.

The peace wasn't loud. It wasn't something he could grasp or hold. It was soft, gentle, the kind of peace that comes when you've finally stopped running from yourself.

He leaned back, looking up at the sky, letting the vastness of the world meet the quiet within him. And in that moment, Noah knew—he wasn't fixed, he wasn't whole, but he was alive. And that was enough.

The tear, the smile, the cloud—all of it was just feeling. And that was all he needed to know.

PART 9: STILL WATERS
A Return to Nature – The Cabin at the Lake

Noah drove for hours, not following a map, but the subtle pull of something inside him. The journey was unmarked, the way undefined—no exact destination in mind. Just open roads that led him further from the pulse of city life and closer to the quiet he'd been craving.

Mira had said it simply, as if it were the most natural thing in the world: "Go where there's nothing to do." And so, here he was, in a place where nothing could be done but be.

The cabin was small, nestled at the edge of a still lake, its weathered wood blending so seamlessly into the forest that Noah had to take a moment to find it. A scattering of wildflowers dotted the ground near the door, and a light mist hovered over the water, a soft veil that made everything feel delicate, sacred, like it could all disappear at any moment. The silence was thick and immediate, the kind that settles into the bones, wrapping around the quiet pulse of nature.

The moment Noah stepped out of his car, he felt his body shift, almost imperceptibly. The tension he hadn't known he carried loosened. He let out a breath that he hadn't realized he'd been holding, and his shoulders dropped from their habitual perch of strain. There was nothing here. No expectations. No demands. Only trees, water, and the vast sky above him, blue and endless.

He took his time settling into the small cabin, no rush, no checklist. The inside was cozy, simple—a bed tucked beneath a window that framed the lake like a painting, a small wooden table with chairs, and an old armchair by the fireplace. The cabin smelled faintly of pine and woodsmoke, as though it had been waiting for him, patiently, for years.

Noah found a kettle, filled it with water, and set it on the stove. He moved slowly, not trying to accomplish anything, just existing in the space. Every movement felt deliberate, grounded—his hands gently finding their way around the rhythm of the cabin.

Outside, the lake shimmered in the early afternoon sun, its surface calm, barely stirred by a light breeze that danced across the water in playful ripples. He opened the door and stepped onto the porch, his bare feet sinking slightly into the wooden floorboards. The air smelled fresh, clean, like it had just been washed, and the only sound was the occasional call of a bird or the soft rustling of leaves as the wind moved through the trees.

No cell service. No clocks. No reminders of who he was supposed to be, or what he was supposed to do. For the first time in a long while, Noah felt as if he could simply *be*.

The first day passed without much thought. He spent hours sitting by the lake, his legs dangling over the edge, watching the water. It was mesmerizing, how still it was, how quiet the world became when you allowed yourself to simply be in it, without needing to control or define it. The water became his mirror, and in its stillness, Noah saw his own reflection—not the one with all the layers, the stories, the old pains—but just him. Quiet. Unspoken. Unrushed.

As the sun dipped below the horizon, he sat in front of the cabin, the air growing cooler as night approached. He wrapped his arms around his knees, feeling the earth beneath him, grounding him in ways he hadn't known he needed.

It was as if the whole world had paused here, waiting for Noah to take his time, to rest and simply exist.

The night sky unfolded like a story, the stars scattered across it in gentle patterns. Noah had forgotten how bright the stars could be, how deeply they could draw you in when you allowed yourself the space to look at them. They felt timeless, unwavering, like they had been there long before him and would remain long after. There was something in their constancy that soothed him—made him feel small, but in a way that felt humbling, not insignificant.

He sat there for hours, wrapped in the stillness, allowing it to fill him up, to replenish what had been drained over the months of emotional work. There was no rush now. No rush to heal or to figure it out or to move on. Everything was just... here.

As the evening deepened, Noah finally went inside. The fire crackled softly in the stove, and he set his things down without urgency. He made a simple meal—vegetables, a piece of bread—and ate slowly, savoring the quiet of it. The solitude felt like a balm, a gift. He didn't feel the need to talk, or to solve anything. Just to be.

He sat by the fire afterward, feeling the warmth of the flames against his skin, and allowed himself to simply exist. The world, for now, was enough. The stillness, the lake, the trees—they were enough. He was enough.

And as he closed his eyes later that night, feeling the softness of the bed beneath him, Noah realized something profound: it wasn't the answers he had been seeking that mattered. It was the capacity to simply live with what is. To exist, without needing to force meaning onto every moment.

No story. No striving. Just being.

The Rhythm of Solitude – Listening Without Seeking

The mornings at the cabin began slowly, without agenda or expectation. Noah awoke each day with the soft light filtering through the trees, casting gentle shadows across the floor. The air felt cool and crisp, but not uncomfortable, just enough to remind him that nature was alive and moving. The first sound he heard each morning was the birdsong—gentle and constant, like an old lullaby sung by the earth itself.

He made tea each morning, but there was no rush in it. No thought of what came next or of any task left undone. He simply watched the steam rise from his cup, listened to the quiet rhythm of the water swirling in the kettle, and let himself settle into the stillness. The tea, once brewed, felt like an offering to himself—warm, fragrant, and slow. He would sit by the window, cup in hand, and look out at the lake, watching the way the early light turned the water to liquid gold.

It wasn't that the silence was deafening, but rather that it was expansive. It invited him to be more present, to see the world without rushing past it. He didn't think about his next step, his next thought, or the world outside. The stillness didn't demand anything from him. It simply *was*.

The lake, still as glass in the mornings, rippled in delicate waves whenever the wind touched it. Noah would sit on the porch, watching these ripples form and fade, and he'd feel himself soften with each passing movement. He realized, in a quiet part of his mind, that the lake mirrored him. His emotions were like those waves—sometimes calm, sometimes stormy—but always, eventually, stilling into a sense of peace.

He took long walks along the shore, barefoot, feeling the coolness of the earth under his feet. Moss clung to the trunks of trees, soft and spongy, like the earth itself was alive and breathing with him. Every step he took felt different from the last. There was no destination—just walking for the sake of walking, noticing the texture of the ground beneath him, the crunch of leaves underfoot, the scent of pine and damp soil.

There were no profound realizations on these walks, no breakthroughs or moments of insight. There was only the wind through the trees, the call of distant birds, and the simple act of moving through the world. Noah's heart began to slow in the stillness, and his mind followed suit. The thoughts that had once crowded in—those constant questions, doubts, and concerns—felt farther away, like the distant sound of traffic that no longer held his attention.

As he wandered deeper into the forest, Noah noticed the details he had once overlooked. The curve of tree bark, the way it spiraled up toward the sky like a winding staircase. The way the light shifted through the leaves, casting shadows that danced across the ground. The softness of the earth underfoot, where tiny wildflowers peeped through the moss, their bright colors catching his eye like forgotten treasures.

He tasted wild berries, sweet and tart, right from the bushes by the cabin. Each one, small and imperfect, reminded him of the beauty in simplicity. There was no rush in the eating, no need to categorize or evaluate. Just the berry, the moment, and the quiet pleasure of it.

Each day, Noah allowed himself more of this: the act of simply being. There was no pressure to fix anything or to analyze his feelings. He had no agenda other than to experience life as it was, in all its small, quiet ways. There was something about it that felt sacred—like he had finally allowed himself to be part of the world again, without the need to control or reshape it.

One morning, after a walk by the lake, Noah stood still for a moment, the soft morning breeze ruffling his hair. His bare feet, cool from the grass, were grounded firmly in the earth. He let himself breathe in deeply, savoring the crispness of the air. For the first time in a long while, he felt something that wasn't a thought, wasn't a plan—it was just a feeling. A soft, silent understanding that he was, simply, enough.

As he stood there, he whispered to himself, as though acknowledging something he had only just realized: "I didn't know peace could feel like this." The words were quiet, but they felt true, a realization that had settled into him in the most gentle of ways. Peace wasn't something to strive for or chase—it was something that simply *was* when he stopped trying to outrun it.

That was the rhythm of solitude that Noah was beginning to discover. It wasn't about learning, fixing, or even improving. It was about being. It was about allowing himself the space to simply exist, to feel the air on his skin, to notice the leaves as they fluttered in the wind, to feel the warmth of the sun on his face without needing it to mean anything other than what it was.

And in that rhythm, Noah began to feel like home to himself. Not in a grand, dramatic way, but in the quietest of shifts. The pressure to become something else, something more, had slipped away. All he had to do now was be here, now, in this moment, and let the world unfold around him.

There was peace in the knowing that, for once, there was nothing he needed to fix. Nothing he needed to strive for. Just this: the rhythm of the world and his own heartbeat, both perfectly in tune with each other.

A Conversation with Silence – The Voice Within

Noah sat by the lake for hours, his back pressed against the rough bark of a tree, legs stretched out in front of him. The air had turned warm in the afternoon sun, but the coolness of the water nearby kept the heat from feeling oppressive. The surface of the lake was smooth, like glass, its stillness mirroring the quiet that had settled within him.

He didn't expect anything. No deep thoughts or revelations. He didn't even try to clear his mind or find meaning in the moment. There was nothing to chase here. No agenda. Just the simple act of sitting, watching, being. The only sounds were the distant calls of birds and the occasional rustle of leaves as a breeze passed through. The silence didn't feel heavy or expectant—it simply *was*.

He let his eyes drift across the water, the surface reflecting the sky in delicate ripples, untouched by the wind. The quiet stretched out before him, wide and open. There was no need to fill it with words, no desire to make it something it wasn't. For the first time in a long time, Noah realized he wasn't fighting with the silence. He wasn't trying to make it into anything.

And then, in the soft space between breaths, something stirred. It wasn't a voice that interrupted the stillness—it was more like a recognition. A thought, simple and clear, surfaced from the deep well of his being, a quiet truth that he hadn't expected. It wasn't dramatic or urgent. It didn't demand his attention with grandiosity or force.

"You don't have to be more. Just be."

The words lingered in the air for a moment, subtle but undeniable. They didn't echo in his mind, but settled into the marrow of his bones. It was a quiet invitation—a reminder, really—that he didn't need to push or strive anymore. He didn't need to be anyone other than who he was, right in this moment.

The message wasn't grand, wasn't life-changing in the way he had once imagined epiphanies to be. But there was something sacred about it. Something *human* in the simplicity of the realization. He had spent so much of his life fighting, resisting, wanting to be something else. But here, in the stillness, there was nothing to fight. There was only the breath of the world moving around him, and the understanding that he didn't need to make anything happen. Life was already happening—he was already part of it.

Noah didn't know how long he sat there, but when he finally stood, his body felt grounded in a way it hadn't before. The air was still warm, the sky still stretched above him, but something had shifted. The silence wasn't empty, as he had once thought it to be. It was full. It was rich with everything that needed to be. It didn't require anything from him, and yet, it gave him everything.

Later that night, as he sat by the small table inside the cabin, Noah picked up his journal, the ink of his pen flowing smoothly across the page. He wasn't sure what to say at first, but the words began to come, gently, without effort:

"Stillness is not the absence of movement. It's the presence of everything."

The journal page seemed to hold his truth for him, a place where all the quiet revelations could be written, solidified in black and white. It wasn't a declaration—it was just the understanding that, in that silence, Noah had discovered something essential. Something he hadn't known he was looking for.

As he closed the journal and set the pen down, Noah leaned back in his chair, letting the quiet of the cabin settle around him like a blanket. He didn't feel the need to rush forward. He didn't feel the weight of time pressing on him. For the first time, he simply *was*. And that, in itself, was enough.

Nature as Mirror – The Lake Teaches Him

Noah stood by the edge of the lake again, drawn to its stillness. The water stretched out before him like a mirror, reflecting the wide expanse of sky above—soft blues and pale clouds drifting lazily by. The lake, in its quiet vastness, seemed to carry no hurry, no rush to be anywhere other than where it was. It was an expanse of perfect peace.

He studied it intently, the smooth surface that held the sky. It was calm, undisturbed, as if it could go on like this forever—unbroken, unmoving. Noah felt the pull of that quietude. He felt the resonance of it in his bones. In his heart. This was peace. Not something he had to chase, or work for, but something that existed simply because the lake allowed it to be. There was an acceptance in the way the water met the air, a surrender to the moment.

But then, as if to remind him that even stillness has its movements, Noah reached down, picking up a smooth stone from the earth. It felt cool in his hand, solid and real. He held it for a moment, turning it between his fingers, and then tossed it into the water with a small arc.

The impact was subtle—just a soft plunk. But the stone disturbed the surface, and in its wake, ripples spread outwards in perfect concentric circles. Noah watched, mesmerized, as the ripples spread farther and farther, like the echo of a thought that traveled through time.

He stood in silence, observing. He realized how natural the ripples were. The lake, in all its calm, didn't resist being disturbed. It didn't fight the stone. It simply responded, adjusted, and then returned to its stillness. It always returned. The disturbance didn't make the lake any less itself—it was only a momentary shift before it returned to peace.

A thought crossed Noah's mind: *I can be stirred, and still return to peace.*

He took a deep breath, letting the metaphor settle in. His life had often felt like that lake, with everything happening around him, shaping him, and pulling him in different directions. He had been like that stone, casting ripples on the surface of his own mind and heart. Fears, pain, anger, joy—each emotion had made its mark. He had felt, at times, like his life was nothing more than a series of ripples—endless and without rest.

But now, standing there, he understood something he hadn't before. The ripples didn't define the lake. They were temporary. Fleeting. And when they passed, the lake would always return to its stillness. Noah could be stirred—he could feel everything, all the emotions that had once felt so overwhelming—but he could still return to peace.

He watched the ripples fade away, the water smoothing out once again. The lake wasn't broken by the disturbance. It simply was. And then it was not.

The breeze picked up slightly, ruffling the surface, but Noah didn't need to chase the peace anymore. He felt it rise naturally, from the core of who he was. He had, at last, found the ability to let things move through him without needing to fix them, or to stop them from happening.

With a quiet sense of wonder, he sat down by the shore, allowing the image of the lake to become a part of him. It wasn't just a body of water—it was a reflection of his own journey, his own evolution. Every ripple, every wave, every moment of disturbance was just another part of the process, another way of becoming who he was meant to be. The lake, with its depths hidden beneath the surface, was always there, still, peaceful, even in the midst of change.

He smiled softly, picking up his journal again as the sun began to set, casting the world in warm golden light. He wrote quietly, with the weight of the lesson sinking deep into his soul:

"Still waters are not without depth."

And as the last light of the day flickered across the lake, Noah understood that the depths within him were not something to fear. They were where his peace lived—beneath the ripples of everything that had passed, was passing, and would pass. And like the lake, he would always return to stillness, again and again, no matter what stirred the surface.

An Unexpected Visitor – A Gentle Reminder

The morning sun filtered softly through the trees, casting long shadows across the cabin's porch. The air was cool, with a touch of dew still clinging to the grass. Noah sat in his favorite wicker chair, the same spot where he had spent countless hours watching the world wake up, sipping tea, and listening to the sounds of nature. Birds chirped in the distance, and the breeze rustled the leaves of the trees like a whisper.

There was no rush. No agenda. No pressure to do anything other than simply be. The silence around him felt expansive, comforting—a space that allowed him to breathe fully without the weight of expectation.

As he sat there, holding his cup of tea, he heard the faint sound of footsteps approaching. His first instinct was to brush it off. The cabin was remote—there was no one around for miles. But the sound came closer, and before he could even rise to see who it was, a figure appeared on the path leading to the cabin.

It was Eden.

She was barefoot, of course, her dark hair flowing gently around her face as she walked with a relaxed grace. Noah's heart gave a soft, surprised lurch at the sight of her—he hadn't expected a visit. But there she was, as if she'd simply felt the pull of the quiet, the same way he had.

She offered him a warm smile, one that reached her eyes and seemed to hold a quiet understanding. No words were exchanged as she took a seat on the porch, just beside him, the sun casting soft highlights on her hair.

For a few moments, they sat in the shared space of silence. The wind stirred the trees, and the air between them was unbroken by conversation. There was no need for words—just a quiet presence that wrapped around both of them like a gentle embrace.

Eden glanced at the teapot beside Noah, then at the cup in his hands, and with a soft laugh, she reached for the kettle. "Would you mind?" she asked, and Noah nodded, pouring her a cup.

They drank in silence, each sip of tea adding to the sense of peace that had already settled over the morning. There was no agenda. No deep conversation waiting to unfold. No rush to fill the quiet with words.

After a time, Eden stood up and gestured toward the lake. "Would you like to skip some stones?" she asked.

Noah felt a lightness in his chest. A soft smile curved on his lips. "I haven't done that in years," he admitted. The simplicity of the act—the feel of the smooth stone in his hand, the weightless moment before it hit the water—felt unexpectedly grounding.

The two of them walked down to the water's edge, and together, they skipped stones across the lake. The sound of the stones landing with a soft splash in the water was a small, rhythmic symphony, a song of quiet connection without words. They didn't need to talk, didn't need to explain anything. The motion of their hands, the arc of each stone, and the occasional laugh as a stone sank too quickly or flew too far, was enough.

After a while, Eden stopped, leaning against a large rock near the shore. She looked at Noah with an expression that was both serene and knowing. "Stillness," she said softly, "isn't loneliness. It's connection."

Noah paused, the thought sinking into him like a pebble in the water. He had spent so many years thinking that stillness and solitude meant being alone. That peace required earning it, somehow—that it was something to be fought for, attained. But here, in this moment, surrounded by nature, with Eden beside him and the soft presence of the lake stretching out before them, he realized that stillness was never about isolation. It was about presence. About being fully alive, fully here, in the moment.

He turned to her, his gaze steady. "I used to think I had to earn peace," he said quietly. "But now... I think peace was always available. Waiting for me to slow down enough to feel it."

Eden smiled, a gentle, knowing smile. She didn't say anything more, but in her eyes, Noah saw the quiet validation of his realization. No need for more words. The truth had already been spoken—between them, and within him. Peace didn't have to be earned. It was already here, just waiting for him to stop running long enough to notice it.

They stayed there for a while longer, skipping stones and sitting in comfortable silence. Time passed without urgency, and Noah felt the weight of the world slip from his shoulders. Not because anything had been solved or fixed—but because he had simply allowed himself to be. With Eden. With the lake. With the soft hum of the earth beneath his feet.

In that moment, Noah realized that peace was never a destination. It was a choice—a choice to simply be, to feel, and to exist within the stillness. And he didn't need to be alone to experience it. Peace and connection, solitude and togetherness, could coexist. All of it was waiting for him, in every moment.

As the sun dipped lower in the sky, casting the world in warm golden hues, Noah allowed himself to savor the moment. He no longer had to seek peace—it was simply a part of him, already there, nestled in the quiet of his heart.

And for the first time in a long time, Noah felt whole.

The Closing Reflection – Peace Without Permission

The cabin felt emptier as the day wore on. Noah stood at the small wooden table, his backpack open in front of him. His things were gathered—clothes folded neatly, a few simple items from the kitchen packed away—but something about the task felt different now. There was no rush, no frantic energy, no need to hurry. It was simply the act of leaving, and yet it didn't feel like departure.

Outside, the lake mirrored the sky, calm and unbroken. The birds that had sung their songs in the morning were quiet now, leaving only the faint rustling of leaves in the breeze. It was as though the world had settled into its own slow rhythm, and Noah was learning to match it.

He paused for a moment, his hand resting on the open journal, feeling the weight of the words he had written just the night before. He had already packed the journals, but this one still lay open beside him, as though it were waiting for something.

Taking a deep breath, Noah dipped his pen into the ink and began to write:

"I came here looking for peace. I found myself. I am the stillness I sought."

The words came easily, not as a conclusion, but as a simple truth. There was no sudden revelation, no grand epiphany. It wasn't about what he had learned or what he had fixed. It was about what he had allowed himself to feel. What he had allowed himself to be.

He smiled softly as he set the pen down. The stillness wasn't just something he found here, at the edge of the lake. It was already inside him—waiting to be recognized. Waiting to be lived.

Noah stood, stretching slowly, then walked to the window. The lake stretched before him, vast and quiet, as if it too were part of him now.

He didn't need to take anything from this place to remember it—yet something still called to him.

He stepped outside, feeling the earth beneath his feet, and wandered down to the water's edge. There, just near the rocks, lay a small stone, smooth and round. It felt right in his palm, solid yet light. He picked it up and turned it over in his fingers, feeling its cool surface, the weight of it grounding him in this moment.

Noah slipped the stone into his pocket, a quiet reminder of the stillness that had become his. He didn't need much—just this small token, a simple connection to the peace he had found within himself.

The sun had begun to dip low, casting long shadows across the ground, but the light still held warmth. The sky was clear, the colors soft and gradual as the day moved toward evening. It felt like a slow exhale, a closing of a chapter, but not an ending. No, this was a beginning. A beginning of living in the peace he had so long sought, not as something outside of him, but as something within.

Noah walked back to the cabin, feeling the weight of the stone in his pocket. He wasn't running anymore, not from the world or from himself. He was simply moving forward—slow, steady, with the quiet certainty that the stillness he sought would follow him. It would be with him, not as something he needed to find, but as something he had become.

With a final glance at the cabin, Noah closed the door behind him and headed down the path, the quiet lake fading behind him. He didn't feel the need to hurry. There was nowhere to go. The world was wide and waiting, but it was no longer a place to fear.

He wasn't escaping it. He was ready to re-enter it, from peace—not pain.

As he walked, the calm sky stretched above him, the air cool and still. The gentle breeze carried with it the scent of pine and earth, and for the first time in a long while, Noah felt completely at home in it.

He was peace.

And that was enough.

The sky lingered in its quiet beauty as Noah walked on, a slow fade into the distance—just a man, at peace with himself and the world.

PART 10: THE GIFT OF VULNERABILITY

The Invitation – A Message from Eden

Noah sat on the couch, the late afternoon light spilling through the window, casting soft, golden hues across the room. It had been a week since he'd left the cabin, and the stillness he'd found there still lingered inside him. His hands rested loosely on his lap, his journal tucked beside him—a symbol of the space he had made for himself. A space of quiet and peace.

The phone buzzed on the coffee table.

He reached for it without thinking, his fingers brushing against the screen. The name that appeared made his chest tighten: *Eden*. He hadn't spoken to her since the retreat, but something about her name still felt like a soft anchor in a storm.

Opening the message, he read the words carefully:

"I don't know where you are in your journey, but I'm holding space if you want to talk."

Noah's heart beat a little faster, not with anxiety, but something gentler, softer. It was like a door creaking open inside of him. He let the words sit with him for a moment, his mind flickering between thoughts—memories of their conversations, of the quiet moments in the garden, of how deeply she had seen him without judgment.

She was offering him something. Not answers, not solutions—but space. Space to be himself, to be seen. A small, but powerful act of trust.

He exhaled slowly, his fingers hovering over the keyboard as he considered how to respond. It wasn't just about the words—it was about what he was willing to let her see. The rawness he had felt at the cabin, the tenderness he had allowed himself to experience in solitude—it was all still with him. But the question now was: would he risk letting someone in to witness it?

He took a breath and typed:

"I'd like that."

There it was—the smallest of commitments, the gentlest of invitations. The words weren't grand, but they felt like a moment of truth, a step forward into the unknown. He hit send before his mind could catch up with him.

The anticipation in the air felt thick, almost like the calm before a storm. He set the phone down and leaned back, staring at the ceiling. For the first time in a while, he allowed himself to feel the weight of his vulnerability. It wasn't just about talking—it was about being seen.

He couldn't predict what would come next. Maybe it would be an easy conversation. Maybe it would challenge him in ways he didn't expect. Either way, something inside him knew: this wasn't about fixing anything. This was about connection. About letting someone see him—not just in the aftermath of pain, but in the wholeness of what he was becoming.

He smiled softly, a quiet warmth spreading through his chest. The fear that had flared up when he first read Eden's message was beginning to settle, replaced by a quiet hope.

This, too, was part of the journey. The invitation to be seen. The invitation to trust.

He didn't know what would come of it, but for the first time in a long while, he was ready to find out.

The phone buzzed again, a new message flashing across the screen.

Eden:

"Let me know when you're ready."

Noah stared at the words for a moment, feeling a lump rise in his throat. He wasn't ready yet—not fully—but he didn't have to be. He would take it one step at a time. And right now, that meant responding to the invitation, allowing himself to step into the light of vulnerability, and trusting that he was worthy of being seen.

For the first time in a long while, he didn't feel the need to hide.

The park was quiet, the air crisp with the lingering coolness of early spring. Noah had arrived early, finding a bench beneath a large oak tree, its leaves just beginning to unfurl in delicate shades of green. Birds sang from high branches, the rhythm of their calls almost a lullaby, soothing the last remnants of tension in his chest. The scent of damp earth and fresh grass filled the air. He breathed deeply, his body settling into the calm that had begun to inhabit him ever since the cabin.

Eden arrived a few minutes later, walking slowly down the path. Her presence was like a quiet breeze, gentle yet unmistakable. She wore a light scarf, its soft fabric moving with the wind, and a warm smile that reached her eyes. When she saw him, her expression softened even further, and she approached with a calm, open energy that immediately put him at ease.

They greeted each other with a quiet hug, one of those simple, comforting moments where words weren't necessary. Eden sat next to him on the bench, the space between them welcoming and unhurried.

For a while, neither of them spoke. Noah watched as Eden reached for a small thermos tucked in her bag, pouring them both tea. The scent of chamomile and lavender filled the air, a softness that matched the atmosphere of the park around them. Everything felt slow—no rush, no need to fill the silence.

Eden took a sip, her eyes never leaving Noah's face, as though waiting for him to find the words, but not pressuring him. She simply held space, her presence like a steady anchor. Noah felt the weight of his own silence, but it wasn't heavy. It was familiar. Safe.

Finally, after what felt like an eternity of comfortable quiet, he spoke, his voice low but steady. "I've been thinking a lot about the lake... about everything that happened there. The stillness. The peace I found."

Eden nodded, her gaze gentle. "It's a beautiful place to find that kind of peace," she said softly. "And sometimes, that stillness isn't just about being away from the noise. It's about reconnecting with ourselves, isn't it?"

Noah leaned back, looking out across the park. "It's more than that," he said, his fingers idly tracing the rim of his teacup. "I thought I was just escaping... But what I realized is that the silence there was just... me. Not hiding. Not running. Just... being."

He paused, feeling the weight of his own words. The quiet of the moment felt sacred, as though the world was holding its breath, giving him space to let the truth rise from deep inside. He swallowed before continuing. "It wasn't just about healing from the past. It was about accepting that I am not just the sum of all my struggles. I'm... more than that."

Eden smiled, a small, knowing smile. She didn't interrupt, didn't rush him to reach the next sentence. She simply waited.

Noah felt a flutter in his chest—something he hadn't expected. A longing, not for something outside himself, but for connection. For shared truth. He shifted slightly, his eyes meeting hers. "I've always shown the strong parts of me first. But lately... the softest parts feel strongest."

The words were out before he could stop them, and as soon as they left his lips, he felt a weight lift. It was as if he had been holding something tender inside, something fragile, and now, at last, he could let it breathe.

Eden's smile deepened, her eyes warm. "That's where the real you lives," she said softly, her voice like a balm. There was no judgment, no expectation. Only a deep understanding, as if she had seen the quiet strength in him all along.

Noah took a slow breath, his chest expanding as he exhaled. The park around them seemed to exhale, too. The sunlight filtering through the leaves felt warmer, softer. And in that moment, he realized something profound: he wasn't just coming to terms with himself in silence. He was learning to share that softness, to trust that being vulnerable didn't make him weaker—it made him whole.

The conversation drifted, flowing easily now, as Noah began to talk about his father, the unresolved tension between them, and the strange release he had found in letting go of the need for resolution. He spoke of Mira, of the grief ritual, and the way he had learned to let emotions simply *be* without judging them.

Eden listened, her presence like the roots of a tree—solid, unshakeable. She didn't rush him to conclusions. She didn't offer advice unless he asked. She simply let him speak, holding the space with such quiet strength that Noah felt more seen in this moment than he ever had before.

As the afternoon passed and the sun began to dip lower in the sky, Noah felt something inside of him soften even more. It wasn't just about what he had shared; it was about the act of sharing itself. The trust. The truth. And the peace that had bloomed, so quietly, in the stillness between them.

The moment stretched on, gentle and open. Eden didn't need to say anything more. She had already given him the most precious gift: the ability to show up, not just with his strength, but with the parts of himself that were still growing, still soft.

He was learning that vulnerability wasn't a weakness. It was a doorway. And right now, in this moment, he had taken one more step through it.

The following days felt different. At first, it was subtle—a slight tightening in his chest when he thought about Eden, a subtle avoidance when he considered how open he had been with her. The connection had been beautiful, but now there was a flicker of panic he hadn't expected.

Noah found himself retreating into silence. The weight of his vulnerability settled on him like a heavy cloak, and he couldn't shake the feeling that he had shown too much. His thoughts began to spiral.

What if I've said too much? What if she sees all the cracks, all the things I'm not?

He closed his eyes and imagined her eyes on him—the way they had softened when he spoke, the understanding in her smile. Yet now, all he could feel was the echo of her gaze, too intense, too searching. *What if I'm too much?* The question gnawed at him.

The moments of peace he had so carefully cultivated in the past weeks now felt fragile, like the calm before a storm. He thought of the lake, of the stillness he had come to trust, and then the waves of uncertainty crashed over him again.

Noah didn't return Eden's messages immediately. He couldn't explain why—there was nothing wrong, nothing had happened. But the space between them had become charged with his own internal conflict.

What if she sees all my faults? What if she leaves because I'm not enough?

The thought hung over him, growing louder each time he tried to push it away.

It wasn't that he didn't want to see her, or talk to her, or share more. It was that the fear of being truly seen—of being loved for who he really was—was so much scarier than he had anticipated. What if she knew everything? What if his brokenness, his fear, his deep-seated insecurity was too much for her to hold?

The tension between wanting to reach out and pulling back became unbearable. He found himself pacing in his small apartment, trying to push away the discomfort in his chest.

Late one night, after hours of tossing and turning, he reached for his journal. His fingers traced the pages, the familiar weight of the notebook grounding him in the stillness. His eyes fell on the words he had written just days before, when he had first realized the strength of his own vulnerability:

"Love doesn't demand perfection. It requires presence."

The words struck him with a force that stopped the whirlwind of his thoughts. Presence. That was what he had shared with Eden—the real, raw presence of himself, not hiding, not pretending. It wasn't about being perfect. It was about showing up, even in the broken places. And maybe that's what made it so terrifying—because in that moment of truth, he had been fully exposed.

He stared at the words, letting them sink in. There was no demand for perfection in love. Just the willingness to be seen, to be present. That was enough. He was enough.

The realization settled over him like a soft wave, and he knew what he had to do. The fear wouldn't go away instantly, and it wasn't about waiting until it disappeared. It was about returning from the retreat, consciously and with intention. He couldn't avoid the discomfort anymore. He couldn't let it control him.

With a deep breath, Noah picked up his phone. His thumb hovered over Eden's contact. He stared at it for a moment longer than necessary, feeling the familiar anxiety rise. But this time, he didn't back away. He tapped out a simple message:

"I've been quiet for a couple of days. I'm sorry about that. I'm just... working through some old fears. But I want to be present, with you. I don't want to hide."

He hesitated before sending it, but then clicked the send button. It felt like a small victory—one where he didn't run, didn't shut down, but opened up the door again, even if only a crack.

Noah sat back in the chair, eyes closing briefly as he felt the familiar, bittersweet mix of relief and fear. There was no going back from this moment. But that was the point, wasn't it? He didn't have to be perfect. He only had to be real.

The phone buzzed minutes later. Eden's reply was simple, warm, and unburdened by judgment:

"I'm here, Noah. No rush. I'm glad you're working through it. I'm here for you, always."

He exhaled, the tightness in his chest releasing just a little. He hadn't been abandoned. He hadn't lost her. In fact, she had met him exactly where he was—with kindness, with patience.

And with that, something inside him shifted. The fear of being seen had been real, but the fear of retreating from connection was worse. He didn't want to hide anymore. Not from Eden, and not from himself.

Noah smiled, the weight of his own vulnerability suddenly feeling lighter. He wasn't perfect. He didn't have to be. He just had to be present. And that was enough.

Noah had never been one to invite others into his rawness. He had learned early on to keep his wounds covered, to show only the polished parts of himself—the parts that could be admired, the parts that didn't demand too much attention. But today, something was different. He wasn't sure what had shifted, but he felt the weight of the unspoken truth pressing against him, the truth that he had kept locked away for so long.

It wasn't that he thought Eden would judge him. He knew, somewhere deep inside, that she wouldn't. But the vulnerability still felt like an offering, a risk. A real one.

After days of back-and-forth texts, simple check-ins, and quiet moments spent reflecting, Noah finally decided to reach out. He invited her over to his place, but he didn't make it sound like anything special—just an invitation to be together, no pressure.

When she arrived, he could see in her eyes that she was holding space for him, that she understood something had shifted, that there was something more between them. She wore her familiar smile, warm and knowing, but there was a softness in the air between them, as if they both knew what this moment could be.

Noah didn't waste time with pleasantries. He led her to the small couch by the window, where the sunlight slanted in, casting a soft glow over the room. There were no grand gestures, no deep setup—just two people who had shared quiet moments, and now, it was time to share more.

He sat down beside her, feeling his heart beat just a little faster. Eden didn't push. She just waited.

"I've been thinking," Noah began, his voice a little rougher than usual. "About all the things I haven't said. All the things I've kept to myself. The things I've been too afraid to share."

Eden nodded, her gaze unwavering. She didn't interrupt, just let the silence hold space for him. It was clear she wasn't waiting for him to be ready—she was simply with him, as he was, in this moment.

"I'm not healed," he continued, the words coming out in a rush now, as if the dam had broken and there was no turning back. "But I'm healing. And I want to do it in the open now. I want to let someone see me, see the parts of me that are still... broken. Because I don't want to hide them anymore."

Eden's eyes softened, but she didn't look away. There was no judgment, no pity. Just a quiet reverence. She reached out, placing her hand over his, a simple gesture of connection, but it spoke volumes.

"Tell me, Noah," she said gently, "Tell me what you've been holding on to."

He took a deep breath, his chest tightening. This was the part he had always been afraid of—the part where the pain became real, where the shame of the past and the uncertainty of the present collided. But as he began to speak, something unexpected happened: it wasn't as hard as he thought.

He told her about his father—the expectations, the silence, the way he had never felt enough. He spoke of the moments when he had needed love, but all he got was distance. The way he had tried to earn affection, to prove his worth, but never quite succeeding.

He shared about the loneliness that had defined so much of his life, the feeling of never being seen for who he truly was, and the fear that had kept him locked in his own shell for years. And, as he spoke, he realized that this wasn't just about telling her his story—it was about finally allowing himself to hear it, too.

"I'm scared of being seen," he admitted, his voice cracking for the first time. "Scared that if someone sees me, really sees me, they won't want to stay. But I'm tired of hiding. I can't do it anymore."

Eden's hand tightened around his. "You don't have to hide," she whispered. "Not from me."

For a moment, there was only the sound of their breath, the quiet hum of the world outside the window, and the weight of their shared silence.

And then, gently, Eden spoke, her voice low but steady. "I've been scared too," she confessed. "Scared of my own grief, scared of being too much or too little. I've tried to protect myself, to hold my pain at arm's length, but it doesn't work. It only keeps me from really living."

She paused, her fingers tracing the edge of his hand. "I think... I think we've both been hiding parts of ourselves, waiting for the right moment to be real. But maybe the right moment is now. Right here."

Noah looked at her, really looked at her, and in that moment, he saw her—not just the calm, grounded version of Eden he had come to know, but the woman who carried her own quiet storm, who had fought her own battles, and had come through them not unscathed, but with grace.

"Thank you," he said softly, his voice breaking slightly. "For seeing me."

Eden smiled, a tender, understanding smile. "I've always seen you, Noah. Even when you didn't see yourself."

The air between them felt full now, heavy with unspoken truths, but also light with the freedom that came from sharing them. They weren't fixing each other, didn't need to. They were simply witnessing each other—each scar, each fear, each fragile piece of who they were.

And for the first time, Noah understood: this was what connection looked like. Not perfection, not fixing, but simply being seen. In all his brokenness, in all his fear, in all his longing for something more, he was still worthy of love. And in this moment, he was loved.

He let out a breath he didn't realize he had been holding. "I'm still healing," he repeated, this time with a softness in his voice that felt like acceptance. "But I'm not alone in it anymore."

Eden didn't respond immediately, but her eyes said everything. She was there—present, real, steady.

They sat together, side by side, in the quiet, knowing that this moment—this sacred sharing—was more than enough.

The night air was cool, carrying with it the scent of earth and a hint of damp grass. They sat together on the porch swing, a slight breeze pushing it back and forth in a gentle rhythm. The stars above seemed close, their quiet, steady glow a reminder of the vastness of the world, and yet, in this moment, it felt as though the universe had narrowed down to just the two of them.

Noah was quiet, his gaze fixed on the distant horizon, but inside, something was stirring. He hadn't been expecting it, hadn't planned for it. But as he sat there, in the stillness, a wave of emotion began to rise within him—unexpected and uninvited, but undeniable.

It started as a tightness in his chest, a familiar ache he'd come to know all too well. It wasn't pain, not the raw, jagged kind he had once carried so deeply. No, this was something softer, more subtle. It was the kind of ache that comes from realizing how much he had been holding back. How much he had needed to feel—and how, for so long, he had resisted it.

He didn't know why it was happening now, why the tears were coming. But they were. And this time, he didn't try to stop them. He let them fall, one after another, until they were spilling down his face in quiet waves, as the weight of being fully seen settled into his bones.

Eden, sitting beside him, didn't speak at first. She simply watched him, her presence steady and unwavering, as if she had known this moment was coming. And then, gently, she reached out, her hand brushing against his arm before moving to wrap around his shoulders, pulling him close.

Noah let himself lean into her, his face resting against her shoulder as the tears kept coming. They weren't the tears of grief or of loss, not entirely. They were the tears of release, of surrender. He was letting go of the tight grip he had on himself, the part of him that had never truly let anyone in. And Eden, without hesitation, was simply there to hold him.

She didn't try to soothe him, didn't offer words of comfort or try to make it better. She didn't try to fix anything. She just stayed. Her arms wrapped around him, steady and warm, her breath slow and calm. And in that moment, Noah realized that he wasn't broken. He wasn't lost. He was just... human.

He whispered into the stillness, his voice trembling slightly, "I didn't know it could feel this safe."

Eden's response was quiet, almost reverent. "This is love. Not saving. Not solving. Just staying."

Noah let out a shaky breath, his body relaxing into her touch, the tears slowing, though he didn't wipe them away. He didn't need to. This moment wasn't about fixing anything—it was about being seen, being held, without the need for anything more. And it was enough.

As the night stretched on, their silence deepened, but it wasn't empty. It was full. Full of everything they had shared, everything they had become. For the first time, Noah wasn't afraid of being seen. He wasn't afraid of being vulnerable. Because he realized, in this space, vulnerability wasn't weakness—it was arrival.

The swing moved gently in the night air, their bodies swaying together in time, a rhythm that felt natural, like the heartbeat of the earth itself. No words were needed. Just the simple, profound act of being there, together.

Noah closed his eyes, letting the peace of the moment wash over him, and for the first time, he didn't feel like he had to earn love. He didn't have to prove anything. He was enough, just as he was.

And in the quiet, under the stars, with Eden's arms around him, he finally understood: love wasn't about fixing. It wasn't about having all the answers. It was about being present. And in that presence, something deep and beautiful could grow.

Noah walked slowly down the quiet street, his footsteps soft on the pavement as the cool night air wrapped around him like a blanket. The stars above shone with an almost intimate glow, as if they, too, were witnesses to his quiet transformation. He wasn't in a hurry to reach home; the stillness of the evening felt like the perfect continuation of what he had just experienced—the release, the acceptance, the peace.

He glanced down at the journal in his hands, feeling the weight of it not as a burden but as a symbol. A tool for reflection, yes, but also a record of his journey—his growth, his unraveling, his coming home to himself.

At the quiet intersection, he paused and leaned against the lamp post for a moment, allowing himself to simply breathe. The weight of the night had settled into his bones, but it wasn't the heaviness of unresolved questions. No, this weight was different. It was the weight of truth—the kind that doesn't drag you down, but anchors you to the present.

His thoughts turned inward, back to the space he had shared with Eden. The words they had spoken were still fresh in his mind. But it wasn't the words that lingered most. It was the silence that had followed them—the comfort in just being there, together, without needing to fill the space with anything more. It was something new, something he hadn't known he needed: connection without performance, love without expectation.

And that's when it hit him.

Vulnerability. It wasn't a final step. It wasn't the end of something. It was the beginning.

It was the door. The first real door he had ever opened to intimacy—not just with others, but with himself.

Noah smiled softly, standing there in the middle of the quiet street, his hand slipping into his pocket to pull out the journal. He flipped it open, feeling the familiar weight of the pages beneath his fingertips. His pen moved without hesitation as he began to write:

"The walls kept the pain out. But they kept love out too. I'm choosing doors now. Open ones."

He paused after the words settled on the page. A deep exhale passed through him, the kind that felt like a release, like a quiet surrender. Everything wasn't solved, not yet. But it didn't have to be. What mattered now was that he was choosing something different.

He wasn't closing off any longer. He wasn't hiding from life. He wasn't afraid to feel, or to be seen.

He closed the journal gently and pressed it against his chest, right over his heart. The warmth of the book, the quiet of the night, the light of the stars—all of it felt like a deep, silent affirmation.

Noah placed a hand over his heart, his fingers resting lightly on the warmth there, and whispered softly to himself, "Thank you."

It wasn't just gratitude for the journey. It was gratitude for the softness he had discovered in himself—the kind of softness that had always been there, just waiting to be embraced.

And with that, the world around him felt peaceful, not because everything was perfect, but because it was real. It was his reality. Vulnerable. Open. Alive.

He smiled again, this time with a deep, peaceful knowing. The journey was far from over—but it was unfolding exactly as it was meant to.

And that, in itself, was enough.

PART 11: THE SHIFT WITHIN
Seeing with New Eyes – The Familiar Looks Different Now

Noah steps into the park, his hands tucked in his jacket pockets, the familiar hum of the city blending with the distant sound of children playing. It's the same park he once avoided, the same bench he sat on during a storm of emotions, eyes glazed with unresolved thoughts. Back then, it was a place of tension, an old haunt that carried memories he didn't know how to process. But today, as he walks under the arching trees, something is different.

The world hasn't changed. He has.

The leaves flutter in the wind, a deeper green than he remembers. The sky feels clearer, as if the clouds themselves have parted, and the sun no longer burns with the harshness it once did. He breathes deeply and notices the warmth of the light on his face, a sensation that once felt oppressive now feels gentle, inviting.

As he passes the café he used to frequent, the smell of coffee doesn't pull at his heart with longing or regret. Instead, it feels like a neutral note in the soundtrack of his day, a reminder of where he's been. His gaze falls on the people sitting at the window—two strangers chatting, their voices soft in the quiet morning. They don't seem so foreign, so distant from the person he once was.

Noah's steps slow. He watches the world move with him, like a dance he's just now beginning to understand. A smile tugs at his lips. He's not in a hurry anymore. He's not running away, or hiding. The old discomforts—those awkward reminders of the past—are still there, but they no longer hold the power they once did.

"The world didn't soften. I did," he thinks, his heart steady, his mind clear. The truth settles in his chest like a gentle weight. Nothing in the world is fundamentally different. But his relationship to it is.

He continues walking, his pace unhurried, enjoying the sounds of the world that feel more alive than ever. The park, the streets, the people—all of it holds new meaning, a more nuanced beauty. And as he moves forward, Noah understands, not with his mind, but with his soul, that the change was never about changing the world. It was always about shifting within.

Noah smiles again, this time with a deeper knowing. Not everything is perfect, but it's real. And right now, that's enough.

Conversations That Flow – Connection Without Performance

Noah stands outside a small café, his hands wrapped around a warm cup of tea, the steam rising into the crisp morning air. He hadn't expected to run into Maya, an old colleague from his previous job. She's the kind of person who exudes quiet confidence, someone who always seemed to have a knack for knowing exactly how to approach a conversation. They hadn't seen each other in months, maybe longer, and when she spots him, she walks over with a friendly wave.

"Hey, Noah! Long time no see," Maya says, her smile easy and familiar.

"Hey, Maya," he responds, offering a small but genuine smile. He doesn't feel the rush to fill the silence, to prove anything in this moment. The conversation, for once, feels effortless. They start with small talk—how things have been, how work is going—but it doesn't feel like a performance, as it once might have. Noah isn't measuring his words or worrying about how he's coming across. There's no script, no agenda. Just a natural flow of exchange.

As they talk, Noah notices something subtle in her demeanor. Her eyes seem to soften when she looks at him, and her voice takes on a warmer tone. Eventually, the topic shifts to more personal ground, and Maya leans in a little, curiosity in her gaze.

"You feel... different," she says, her voice light but observant. "Calmer, maybe?"

Noah shrugs, almost sheepishly, before a soft grin spreads across his face. "I stopped trying to be everything I'm not."

The words come with ease, as though the weight of all those years of pretending, of carrying the burden of someone else's expectations, have finally been put down. Maya's smile deepens, a knowing look in her eyes.

"I like it," she says, her voice warm. "It's like... you're actually here now. Not just going through the motions."

Noah's chest feels lighter at her words. It's not praise. It's not about approval. It's just connection. Real, uncomplicated. No need to perform, no need to hide. He feels the distance between the person he used to be and the person he's becoming—someone who doesn't need to prove worth, someone who can simply exist in his own skin.

They continue talking, the conversation moving seamlessly from one subject to another, with no pressure, no effort to impress. And as they talk, Noah realizes something: it's not just that he doesn't need to prove anything to Maya—it's that he no longer feels the need to prove anything to anyone. Not even to himself.

When they part ways, Maya gives him a hug, and he feels her warmth, the unspoken recognition of the shift in him. For the first time in a long while, Noah walks away from a conversation feeling at peace—not because he's said the right things, but because he's said what's true.

And the truth is, he doesn't need to wear a mask anymore. He can simply be.

The Return to the Journal – This Time, Without Questions

The soft golden light of the late afternoon fills Noah's apartment, casting long shadows across the walls. He sits by the window, his legs stretched out, his back against the chair. The world outside moves at its usual pace—people hurrying down the street, the rustle of leaves in the wind, the distant hum of traffic. But here, in his space, it feels quieter. More settled.

For the first time in a while, Noah feels a pull toward the journal. The one that had been a lifeline during his most difficult moments. The one that had held his rawest thoughts, his deepest fears, and his hardest truths. He had filled its pages with struggles, confessions, and revelations. In its pages, he had sought solace. But today, there is no urgency. No need to fix or search for answers.

He reaches for it, feeling the familiar weight of the leather cover in his hands. The gold lettering on the spine is worn now, the edges of the pages soft from his frequent turning. Opening the journal, he runs his fingers lightly over the pages—tears, scribbles, mantras—all of it a testament to the journey he's walked.

This time, he doesn't feel compelled to write out his pain. He doesn't need to pour out his frustrations, or search for the right words. Instead, he simply lets his eyes drift over the lines, feeling the depth of each word, each sentence, not as a problem to be solved, but as a record of who he was and who he's becoming.

Noah flips through a few pages, stopping on the entry where he first wrote the words that had stayed with him: *"Feeling is not weakness. Feeling is witnessing."* He smiles softly, remembering how hard it had been to believe that at first. He recalls the weight of the grief, the shame, the fear that had threatened to consume him. But now, those emotions no longer feel like chains. They feel like chapters in a story he's learned to embrace.

He moves to another page, where he had written one of Mira's teachings: *"Forgiveness isn't saying it didn't hurt. It's saying I won't be hurt by it anymore."* He reads it slowly, allowing the words to settle in him once more. He doesn't need to search for forgiveness anymore. It's already within him, quiet and steady, like a river that's learned to flow around obstacles instead of fighting them.

As his eyes move from one page to the next, he comes to the final line he wrote not long ago:

"I am a sky wide enough for every kind of weather."

And now, with a deep exhale, Noah writes something new.

"It's no longer about fixing. It's about flowing."

The words come easily, effortlessly. He pauses, reflecting on them. It's not about changing anything anymore, about controlling the storm inside. It's about learning to flow with it, to allow it to pass without resistance, to feel each wave without drowning. He doesn't need to force his growth or find the perfect answer. He's learning to trust the process, to trust himself.

Noah closes the journal, but not with the sense of finality he once might have felt. It's not a goodbye. It's more of a quiet acknowledgment. The journal has served its purpose. It helped him listen, helped him find the courage to sit with his emotions, to reflect, to understand. But now, he no longer needs it as a crutch. The wisdom is inside him, embodied, quiet but ever-present.

He places the journal on the shelf, not as something he'll never return to, but as something that's already woven into the fabric of who he is. The journal is no longer a tool. It's a mirror of his transformation.

And in that moment, Noah understands. He's no longer seeking the answers. He's living them.

Mira Returns – A Quiet Affirmation

The air is crisp as Noah walks down the narrow street, his steps in sync with the rhythm of his thoughts. The world feels slower these days—gentler. Each step is a small declaration of his new pace, one that matches the stillness inside him. The past months have been a symphony of transformation, each note resonating with the quiet hum of peace he's learning to carry.

He passes a small bookstore, the kind that smells like old paper and rain. Something about it catches his attention, pulling him inside without thinking. He lets the cool air of the store settle around him, running his fingers over the spines of books. For a moment, he's lost in the quiet familiarity of this place, surrounded by the soft whispers of stories.

As he turns a corner between the shelves, there she is.

Mira. The last person he ever expected to see here, yet somehow, not surprising at all. She's standing by the poetry section, her gaze lost in the pages of a book, her presence just as calm and steady as he remembers. Her energy still carries that same quiet depth—an unspoken understanding that doesn't need to be voiced.

She looks up when he approaches, her face lighting up with a soft smile.

"You've changed," she says simply, the words like a small bell ringing in the stillness of the bookstore.

Noah feels something stir inside him—not an urge to explain or justify, just a simple, deep acknowledgment of the truth she's spoken. He nods, a smile tugging at his lips.

"Yeah," he replies, his voice calm, but full of warmth. "But not into someone new—just into who I always was."

Mira's smile deepens, and she nods as if everything makes sense in that moment. The years, the work, the challenges—it's all led here. To this quiet, gentle recognition of his own transformation.

"That's all the Law of Release ever was," she says softly. "To let go of who you thought you had to be, and to simply become who you already were."

Noah feels the weight of her words settle in him like a soft landing. The Law of Release—it had always been about this: not becoming something different, but allowing himself to remember the truth of who he is, beneath all the layers of fear, doubt, and resistance.

Mira reaches into her pocket and pulls out a small stone, smooth and polished, with a single word etched on its surface.

"Remember," she says, handing it to him with the kind of tenderness that only someone who has witnessed a person's growth can offer.

Noah takes the stone into his palm, the word a quiet promise. A reminder that everything he's learned, everything he's felt, was always meant to be a part of him. Not a lesson to forget, but something to carry forward.

"Thank you," he says, his voice filled with gratitude.

Mira gives a gentle nod, her eyes speaking volumes without a single word. She doesn't need to say anything more. Her work with him is done. The guide has led him to this point, and now, she steps back, not because she's leaving, but because Noah no longer needs a guide.

She turns and walks away slowly, disappearing into the aisles of the bookstore, as quietly as she arrived.

Noah stands there for a long moment, the stone still warm in his hand. He doesn't rush to leave. Instead, he takes a deep breath, letting the peace of this simple encounter fill him. There's nothing left to fix, nothing left to seek. He is already whole.

With a smile, he walks out of the bookstore, the stone tucked safely into his pocket. The world is the same, and yet everything feels different. And for the first time, he knows that he doesn't need to chase after anything. The truth of who he is will always be with him, in every step, in every breath.

Mira's work is done, but the journey continues. And Noah knows that, no matter where he goes, he'll always carry the quiet reminder within him: *Remember.*

The Shift in Relationships – Holding Without Holding On

The sun is gentle on the late afternoon, casting a golden hue over the city as Noah and Eden walk side by side. There's a quiet rhythm to their steps now, a fluidity that comes not from effort, but from ease.

There's no hurry, no need to fill the air with words. Just the sound of their shoes on the pavement and the occasional bird call.

They stop at a park bench, the trees around them swaying lightly in the breeze. Noah sits first, letting his body sink into the simple comfort of the moment. Eden follows, settling beside him without a word, just the quiet hum of shared space between them.

For a while, they don't speak. Instead, they let the peace of their surroundings fill the silence, the warmth of the sun on their skin a gentle reminder that nothing needs to be forced.

Noah thinks about how different this moment feels. There was a time, not so long ago, when silence would have felt like a void to him, something to fill with chatter or distractions. But now, he welcomes it. It doesn't need to be filled, because it already is. He looks over at Eden, her eyes closed as she tilts her head to the sky, and he realizes that he feels no fear of this quiet. Only contentment.

After a while, he speaks, his voice soft but steady.

"I used to think love meant holding on tight," he says, his gaze still on the sky above. "Now I think it means holding space."

Eden opens her eyes, her smile slow but genuine. It's the kind of smile that speaks of deep understanding, of a love that doesn't need to control or possess, but simply to exist. She nods.

"I agree," she says, her voice a quiet murmur. "Love is letting each other breathe, letting each other be."

Noah feels something shift inside him, not just in the space between them, but within himself. It's a feeling of release, as though he's finally exhaled after holding his breath for too long. There's a freedom in their connection now—a freedom from expectations, from fears of abandonment or rejection. They are simply two people, existing together without needing to grasp at each other.

As the afternoon unfolds, they share small moments of joy—Eden laughs at a joke Noah makes, and he finds himself laughing with her, not from any particular need to impress, but because it feels good to simply be in each other's company. They share a sandwich and a few quiet stories from their past, not trying to make the moment anything more than what it is.

It's a dance of freedom, where love is not a force pulling them together, but a current that gently moves them in sync, without pressure or urgency. There's no sense of scarcity in the air, no worry about what will come next. Only the ease of being present, of holding space for each other to simply exist.

Later, as they walk back towards Noah's apartment, he feels lighter. Not because he's let go of something, but because he's allowed himself to be held—held by Eden's presence, by the stillness of the world around them, by the love that no longer demands, but simply is.

He looks at her and smiles.

"I used to think I had to hold on to keep something real," he says quietly. "But now, I see that the realness comes from letting it flow."

Eden squeezes his hand, a silent agreement, and together they walk in the quiet peace they've created—not by holding on, but by holding space for each other to grow, to breathe, to be.

For the first time in a long time, Noah feels deeply in love—not just with Eden, but with life itself. He breathes easier now.

The Mirror Moment – He Sees Himself

Noah walks through the quiet streets, his steps slow, almost meditative. The city around him hums with the usual rhythm of life—people walking, cars passing, the distant murmur of conversation—but for once, he isn't caught in it. He's present. He's not rushing, not trying to be somewhere he isn't. He's just here, in this moment, with the peace he's cultivated within himself.

As he walks past a small boutique, he notices the reflection of the street in the glass window. It's not the kind of reflection that pulls him in for a quick check—there's no self-consciousness, no need to adjust his appearance or check if he looks okay. He doesn't even mean to stop, but something stills him.

He stands there, still for a moment, and looks at his reflection. Not just at the face staring back, but at the person who's been through so much, the person who's been breaking and rebuilding for so long. He doesn't see the cracks, the wounds, the parts that used to feel too fragile to show. Instead, he sees someone whole—someone who has walked through the storms and learned to dance in the rain.

There's softness in his eyes, something tender but strong, and a quiet confidence in the way he carries himself. He's not perfect. He's not finished. But he's real. He's enough. And for the first time, he realizes that he doesn't need to be anything more. He just is.

Noah whispers to himself, so softly it's almost lost in the noise of the world around him:

"You made it through. And you're still soft."

It's not a triumphant moment. There's no grand gesture, no sudden burst of realization. Just a quiet knowing. A quiet acceptance of who he is. He's not chasing anything anymore. He's not running from himself or the world. He's simply present, and for the first time, he feels at peace with that.

He takes a deep breath, and as he exhales, a weight lifts from his shoulders—one he didn't even realize he was carrying. He's not trying to be someone he's not. He's just Noah, standing here, fully met. Fully seen.

With one last glance at his reflection, Noah walks away. Not toward something, but with something—himself. Fully embraced, fully whole. And for the first time, he feels that peace settle deep within him, not as a destination to reach, but as something he's already found.

And in that peace, he takes another step, leaving behind the man he once was and walking forward as the man he's becoming.

PART 12: LIVING THE LAW
Returning Home – A New Presence in Old Spaces

Noah stands in the doorway of his apartment, key still in hand, his body feeling lighter than he expected. The door clicks shut behind him, and for a moment, he just breathes in the familiar space—the worn carpet, the kitchen counter with the small pile of dishes, the quiet hum of the refrigerator. It's the same place he left, the same space he's inhabited for years. But something feels different.

It's not the apartment that's changed—it's him.

There's no rush to fill the space with activity, no urgency to fix the things he's avoided. The clutter that's piled up over months doesn't feel like a weight anymore, just remnants of a past life, waiting to be cleared. The clutter—old magazines, forgotten coffee mugs, books he hasn't read—no longer feels like part of him. It's simply...stuff. And it's time for it to go.

Noah sets the key on the counter and starts moving through the apartment. He picks up an old jacket draped over the chair, folding it with slow, deliberate movements. He tosses aside the shoes left scattered at the door, not out of frustration, but simply to make space. Each action feels intentional, a subtle act of release, as though he's shedding the layers of a life that no longer serves him.

The memories are still here. The faded photograph on the wall. The old record player by the window. Each piece a memory, but none of them possess the same weight they once did. He notices how light the air feels as he moves through the apartment, how the space opens up, how the walls seem to breathe with him.

He walks to the small bookshelf in the corner, his fingers brushing over the spines of the books. They're familiar, some of them worn down by time, others still new. He pulls a few off the shelf, holding them in his hands for a moment before setting them aside—deciding, not out of obligation, but out of ease, that they can go.

It's not about erasing the past. It's about making room for what's next.

Noah smiles quietly to himself as he opens the closet door. Old clothes hang on the rod, some of them never worn, some that no longer fit. One by one, he pulls them down, letting go of them without attachment. He places them in the donation bag, not feeling guilty, not feeling regret. Just...emptying out what's no longer needed.

"Living the Law means living light," he whispers under his breath, the words flowing from him with ease, as though they've always been true.

It's not about letting go of things because they hurt. It's about making space for new energy, new growth, new experiences. The old life is not gone, not erased—but it no longer defines him. His life now is more spacious, more open, and filled with the possibility of something new.

He moves through the apartment with a quiet, steady rhythm, clearing out the old clutter, and in doing so, clearing out the old emotional residue. There's no rush. No hurry. Just a gentle, deliberate motion, one action at a time. His movements are soft, grounded in a peace he's never known before.

By the time he finishes, the apartment feels...different. Cleaner. More open. It's not just the space that's transformed; it's him, too. He sits down on the couch, looking around at the simplicity of the room. The walls feel welcoming now, not suffocating. The furniture feels inviting, not heavy. It's a space that holds him, rather than holds him back.

Noah exhales slowly, his hand resting lightly on his chest. He feels no need to rush into anything, no need to fill the space with noise or distractions. For the first time, he's just here. Just present. He closes his eyes for a moment, feeling the stillness settle around him, and the words come again, this time without hesitation:

"Living the Law means living light."

It's not just the apartment that has shifted. It's him—his internal world reflected outward, creating space for the present moment, for possibility, for peace.

Noah leans back, letting his body settle into the couch. He doesn't need to do anything. He doesn't need to prove anything. He's simply here. Simply at home.

And for the first time in a long while, he feels it. The stillness. The peace. The lightness of being.

It's not a destination, but a way of living. A way of being. And for the first time, Noah feels fully alive in his own space, with no past dragging him down and no future pulling him away. Just the present, unfolding softly in front of him, as if he's seeing it for the very first time.

A New Way to Work – Creating from Flow, Not Force

Noah sits at his desk, staring at the blank screen in front of him. It's a freelance project—design work for a local business that needs branding. He's done this kind of work a thousand times before, but today feels different. His fingers hover over the keyboard, but there's no rush to begin. He's not chasing an outcome, not trying to push an idea into existence.

In the past, he would have been consumed by deadlines, by the need for perfection. But today, he feels no urgency, no pressure. He simply sits with the quiet.

The design concept is there somewhere, he knows it is. But it doesn't need to arrive all at once. He smiles softly as the thought settles in: *I used to chase clarity. Now I let it come.*

He takes a deep breath, leaning back in his chair. The office is quiet. The hum of the city outside is distant, as if muffled by the stillness inside him. He stands up slowly, moving toward the window. He watches the trees swaying in the breeze, their leaves rustling softly in the air. There's no hurry in their movement, no forced direction. They simply sway, existing as they are, in the flow of the present moment.

Noah decides to step outside. He walks barefoot onto the grass in his backyard, feeling the cool earth beneath his feet. The fresh air fills his lungs, and he closes his eyes, letting the stillness of nature ground him. For a few moments, he's not thinking about design, not thinking about deadlines or client expectations. He's just here. Just being.

As he walks through the grass, a spark of inspiration comes. It's not loud or sudden, but gentle—like a soft whisper. An idea, simple and clear, begins to form in his mind. He smiles, feeling the flow of creativity move through him, without effort, without struggle.

Noah pauses, watching a bird glide above him, its wings outstretched, carried effortlessly by the wind. He feels a shift inside him—a deep, quiet understanding. The work he's about to do isn't about proving anything. It's not about creating for approval, for validation. It's about expression. It's about flow.

He returns to his desk, refreshed and open. This time, when he sits down to work, there's no force. No rigid structure. Just a sense of play, of curiosity. His fingers begin to move across the keyboard, and the design takes shape. It's not perfect yet, but it feels right. It feels aligned with something deeper than the need for completion.

He smiles again, this time with a knowing—surrender isn't passive. It's co-creative. It's a dance between him and the idea, a conversation that flows without resistance. The ideas come and go, and he welcomes them without urgency. They come in their own time, and he lets them.

As the design begins to unfold, Noah feels peace. There's no need to prove his worth. No need to force something into being. The work is simply a reflection of the peace he's found within himself. Each stroke, each line, is an expression, not an achievement.

He writes a note to his client later that day, explaining that the design is coming together in a way that feels authentic and free. He doesn't mention the creative process in detail, but it's clear—the work flows from the peace he's discovered. It's not just about the finished product; it's about the space in which it was created.

Noah leans back in his chair, watching the project come to life with ease. For the first time, he realizes that creation is not a race. It's not something to be conquered. It's something to be experienced, something to flow with.

"I create to express my peace," he whispers to himself, the words rolling off his tongue with a quiet truth. He feels the work shifting inside him—not just as an outcome, but as an experience. He's no longer working to fill an empty space. He's creating because, in the act of creation, he feels whole.

Meeting Resistance with Grace – An Unexpected Trigger

Noah walks into the grocery store, the hum of fluorescent lights and the clink of carts filling the space. It's a typical errand, a quiet moment in the midst of his day. As he moves through the aisles, picking out the essentials—bananas, almond milk, pasta—his mind is clear. He's calm, settled in the peace he's been nurturing.

And then, it happens.

He rounds a corner and comes face-to-face with Greg, an old colleague from his previous job. Greg's the type who's always a little too quick with a critique, too eager to make his opinion known. They exchange a brief, polite greeting, but then the words slip out, sharp and unexpected.

"You're looking a little... soft these days, Noah. Guess that's what happens when you take time off, huh? Not everyone can afford to do that."

It's said with that familiar edge of judgment, the same tone that used to trigger something inside Noah—the need to defend, to prove, to fight back. The old reflex kicks in, his heart rate quickening, a small fire of irritation stirring in his chest. For a brief moment, Noah feels the heat rise, his mind already shaping words to retaliate. He could feel his old anger swelling, his defenses already locked in place.

But then, he remembers Eden's words. The stillness of them. Her gentle reminder: *"You don't have to pick up every stone thrown your way."*

He breathes.

The heat of the moment lingers, but it doesn't consume him. He doesn't need to explain himself, doesn't need to prove anything. He simply smiles, a small, unbothered smile, and says, "I guess I'm just learning to enjoy the quiet."

Greg frowns, a brief flicker of confusion crossing his face before he shrugs and walks away, none the wiser. Noah stands there for a moment, watching him go, the small ripples of discomfort fading into the background. He lets it pass. No anger, no defense. Just... release.

He continues with his shopping, a sense of lightness settling over him, and as he walks toward the checkout line, he reflects on the moment, the tension, the release.

Release isn't about being unshaken. It's about not gripping what shakes you.

The words echo in his mind, a gentle affirmation of how far he's come. Noah doesn't feel the need to confront, to engage, to let the old wounds dictate his actions. Instead, he responds with kindness, with softness, and in doing so, he feels a quiet power—the ability to stand without resistance, to remain grounded even when the world tries to push him.

Later that evening, as Noah unpacks his groceries, he feels the subtle shift of the moment—a shift not in the world around him, but in how he holds himself in the world. It's the embodiment of all the work he's done. Peace isn't the absence of resistance; it's the grace with which he meets it.

And as he puts the last of the produce in the fridge, Noah smiles to himself, a quiet, knowing smile. He doesn't need to grip the stones anymore.

Love Without Need – A Conversation with Eden

The morning sun is soft, filtering through the trees as Noah and Eden walk side by side down a quiet city street. The air is crisp, filled with the gentle hum of a city coming to life, but their pace is slow—measured, unhurried. There's no rush. There's no destination they're racing toward. Just two people, in sync with each other and the rhythm of the world around them.

Noah glances over at Eden, her expression peaceful, her steps light. He's realized, over time, that the love they share now is different—deeper, quieter, more rooted in a sense of freedom than anything he had imagined before.

As they walk, they talk—nothing urgent, no heavy conversation, just a sharing of thoughts, an exchange of small moments. Eden brings up a book she's been reading, and Noah adds his own musings on a recent idea he's been working through in his creative project. There's a softness in the way they speak, a mutual understanding that there's no need for anything more than what is.

After a while, Noah speaks again, his voice thoughtful.

"I love that we can love without holding each other hostage," he says, the words unfolding naturally, a quiet truth between them. "There's no need to force anything, no need to make promises or shape what's ahead of us. We're just here, together, as we are."

Eden's smile is gentle, understanding. She turns to him, her eyes full of warmth.

"Because we know now: the more open the hand, the more gently it holds," she responds softly. The words carry weight, but they're not heavy. They're a truth that's been lived, not just learned.

Noah nods, his heart swelling with the quiet depth of what she's said. There's no expectation in their connection now, no fear of loss, no urgency to define what they are or what they will become. It's enough to simply be present in this moment, to love without needing to possess, to trust without fear.

They continue walking, the sound of their footsteps echoing in the quiet morning. The city around them moves, people bustling by, cars driving past, but there's something sacred in their shared space—a space that doesn't demand more than what they already are.

The Law of Release has reshaped the love they share. It isn't smaller or more limited, but freer, more alive. Love isn't a thing to hold tightly to anymore. It's a force they both carry, one that expands with each breath, without the need to grasp.

No future is planned between them—not because they don't care about what's ahead, but because they don't need to. The future is simply lived in each moment, each choice they make together. They don't force anything into being. They just breathe, and in the space between their breaths, everything is as it should be.

Noah feels lighter as they walk, a quiet sense of peace in the way their hands brush occasionally, in the shared silence, in the simple joy of each other's presence. They don't need to define what they have. They don't need to grasp at a future. They are already living it, with open hands and hearts full of trust.

He looks over at Eden, and in that moment, he knows—this is love. Not the kind he once imagined, not the kind that demanded, but the kind that simply is, breathed into being with ease. And he feels deeply, profoundly grateful.

A Creative Offering – Sharing What He's Learned

Noah sits at his desk, fingers resting lightly on the keys of his laptop. He's been here before, writing in search of something—answers, clarity, maybe even validation. But today, there's no urgency in his fingers, no striving in his thoughts. He simply wants to share, to offer what he's learned without expectation.

The words begin to flow as he writes the opening line:

"Here's what helped me. Maybe it will help you too."

He pauses, letting the simplicity of that sentence settle in. There's no need to frame himself as someone with all the answers. No need to be anyone other than the person who's walked a path, stumbled, and found something that feels like peace. He shares a few lines from *The Law of Release*, words that once guided him through the hardest moments of his life:

"Release isn't the absence of struggle. It's the presence of everything—without the need to fix it."

Then he tells the story of the lake, of the quiet mornings spent watching the water ripple with each stone he threw. He talks about Mira and the breath, how it was in the stillness, in the letting go, that he began to see himself clearly for the first time.

"I didn't know peace could feel like this," he writes, quoting his own whispered words from the lake.

He doesn't offer solutions. He doesn't promise that anyone who reads this will find their own lake or their own moment of clarity. He doesn't even ask for anything in return. This is not about teaching, not about being an expert. This is just sharing. Just being real.

After he finishes the post, Noah hits 'publish,' feeling a quiet sense of satisfaction—not from accomplishment, but from a deeper knowing that the offering is enough. He's given it without expectation, without trying to craft anything beyond what was true.

The response comes slowly, and when it does, it's soft. No applause. No grand declarations. But in the comments section, one stands out:

"I didn't know I needed to hear this today. Thank you."

Noah smiles to himself, reading the words again. He doesn't need more than this. The connection, the resonance—it's enough. It always was.

He leans back in his chair, breathing deeply, feeling that familiar stillness wash over him once again. The Law of Release has never been about getting something in return. It's always been about offering what is true, what is real, and letting the rest fall into place.

No ego. No how-to. Just witness.

And as he sits there, in the quiet of his apartment, Noah realizes that this—this simple act of sharing—feels like the most natural thing he's ever done.

Ordinary Magic – A Life That Breathes

The soft light of dawn spills across the kitchen counter as Noah fills the kettle with water, the familiar sound of it humming gently as it heats. He moves quietly, not rushing, not expecting anything extraordinary. The kitchen is simple, the air cool, and the world outside still wrapped in the quiet of morning.

As the steam rises from the kettle, he pulls a small jar of honey from the cupboard, his hand moving naturally, without thought. The light shifts on the wall, painting soft patterns on the cream-colored surface. The birds outside begin to stir, their morning song filling the space.

A sparrow flits to the windowsill, perching for a moment, its small body silhouetted against the pale blue sky. Noah watches it, a gentle smile touching his lips. There's nothing spectacular about the moment—nothing that demands attention. It just *is*.

The kettle clicks off, and he pours the hot water into his favorite mug, the one with a chipped rim he's had for years. He stirs in the honey, the warmth of it filling his hands, his chest, like a quiet comfort.

The faint sound of music plays in the background—something instrumental, soft, just enough to fill the space without demanding it. He lets out a small laugh, the kind that bubbles up unexpectedly. Maybe it's something he thought of, or maybe it's the sheer contentment of being here, in this moment, in this life. Only he knows, and that's enough.

As he sips the tea, he thinks:

"I used to think awakening would feel like lightning. But it feels more like this. Like breath. Like home."

There's no rush, no striving. Just the rhythm of the morning, the simplicity of being present. The feeling that life is happening, not later, not in the future—but right here, right now. He feels the truth of it in his bones, in the quiet joy of this small, ordinary moment.

Noah doesn't need more. He's not waiting for life to begin. It's already begun. He's already living it, each moment unfolding like a breath, a step into something deep and real.

And as the sun continues to rise, casting golden light across the room, Noah closes his eyes for a moment, savoring the peace that surrounds him. He's here. He's home.

The stillness wraps around him like a soft blanket, the quiet, luminous presence of the morning filling every corner of the room.

This is enough. It always was.

PART 13: A CIRCLE COMPLETED
The Letter

Noah's hand paused mid-reach, the rustling sound of paper breaking the quiet in his apartment. A plain, unmarked envelope sat on his doorstep, its edges worn from travel, but the address was his own. No return address. No stamp. He knelt down to pick it up, the weight of the envelope simple, yet carrying a strange gravity.

He turned it over, searching for any sign of who might have sent it, but there was nothing. Just smooth, blank paper. The curiosity stirred in him. With a slow, deliberate motion, he slid his finger under the flap and opened it.

Inside was a single, neatly written line:

"Meet me where you first remembered to breathe."

The handwriting was unmistakable. Mira.

A deep, steady breath filled Noah's lungs. He didn't have to think twice. He knew exactly where she meant. The lake. The same place where he had come undone and slowly rebuilt himself, where the silence had whispered the truth he'd long denied. The lake had been the backdrop of his awakening, and now, it seemed, it was calling him again.

He stood there for a moment, holding the letter in his hands. No questions. No resistance. Just a quiet knowing that this was part of the circle—the journey that had begun at the lake would now come full circle there as well.

Noah packed light, a small bag slung over his shoulder. The lake had never been about the things he brought with him—it was always about what was stripped away. A light jacket, a few essentials, and his journal—everything he needed to complete the journey. The lake had been a place of profound silence, but Noah had learned that even in silence, there was always something to be said. And this time, he felt ready to hear it.

The drive to the lake felt different. In Part 2, when he first came here, he had been lost—full of questions, pain, and unresolved tension. Now, as he drove, the road felt like an old friend, familiar yet new. He was different. The landscape, the trees, the winding path—all felt like they had shifted with him, though he knew they hadn't. He had. The world around him no longer felt overwhelming; it felt like a place he belonged to. There was no urgency, no fear, just a quiet, steady rhythm. A reunion with himself.

Arriving at the lake, Noah didn't immediately search for Mira. Instead, he stood at the edge, gazing out at the still water. The ripples from the gentle breeze were faint, the surface of the lake reflecting the sky like a mirror. He felt the ground beneath his feet, the earth supporting him, steady and unyielding. In this moment, Noah understood something deeper: the lake wasn't a place of transformation—it was a place of remembrance. He hadn't changed. He had only rediscovered who he always was.

The journey here had been a reflection of his evolution. Where he once arrived confused and heavy, he now walked with quiet clarity. His steps were lighter, his heart fuller, and he could feel the shift—he was no longer waiting for something to happen. He was no longer trying to become something. He was simply *being*. This was the grace of the Law of Release: to trust that everything he sought was already within him.

He sat down on the familiar bench by the water, the place where Mira had first spoken to him about release and surrender. His journal rested in his lap, unopened, as if he didn't need it anymore. He could feel the weight of it in his bones, the wisdom of it now part of his being.

The sound of footsteps reached his ears, light and measured. Noah turned, and there she was. Mira. Not as a teacher, not as someone holding answers, but simply as herself—quiet, steady, and present.

She smiled softly when she saw him. "You came."

Noah stood, the air between them thick with unspoken understanding. He nodded. "I did."

Mira's gaze softened as she studied him. "I didn't come to teach you anything. You've already learned."

Noah felt something stir within him—gratitude, humility, a recognition that he had been walking this path all along. She wasn't here to offer him a final lesson. She was here to remind him of what he had already realized, to help him see that the journey he had traveled was never about becoming someone else—it was about remembering who he had always been.

The silence between them deepened, comfortable and full. Mira sat beside him on the bench, the lake lapping gently at the shore in rhythm with their breaths. There was nothing to say, nothing to prove. Just the soft hum of the world around them.

Finally, Mira spoke, her voice low and warm. "The journal was never about finding the right answers, Noah. It was a mirror. You didn't need to fix yourself. You only needed to remember."

He nodded slowly, his heart lighter now. "It wasn't about instruction," he said quietly. "It was about listening."

"Yes," Mira agreed. "And now you are listening—always."

Noah took a deep breath and looked out over the water. The world, once full of noise, now felt profoundly still. He understood now that the stillness wasn't emptiness—it was full of everything that mattered.

Mira's presence, her reminder, felt like the final piece of a puzzle Noah hadn't known he was solving. He hadn't needed to seek the answers. They had always been there, waiting for him to be still enough to hear them.

"I think I understand," Noah said, his voice steady. "It's not about what I do, but about who I am when I do it. It's about releasing everything that's not real so I can remember what's always been."

Mira smiled, her eyes twinkling with quiet pride. "Exactly. You've come full circle, Noah. You've always been whole."

Noah sat there for a moment, allowing her words to settle inside him. The past was no longer a weight he carried—it was simply part of his story. The present, filled with the peaceful clarity of the lake, was all he needed now. He wasn't just living the Law of Release—he was living *from* it.

As the sky above the lake deepened into evening, the two of them sat in companionable silence. There was nothing more to say. Everything was already understood.

And in that moment, Noah knew: he wasn't waiting for anything. He wasn't seeking anything. He was simply *here*. Whole. And everything was enough.

The air around the lake was still, the water holding a quiet sheen under the soft afternoon light. Noah approached the familiar spot, a sense of serenity within him as the path he walked felt not like a return but a continuation—a quiet evolution.

At the edge of the water, Mira stood, as calm as ever. She turned to him, no surprise in her eyes, just a knowing smile that had become a part of her presence.

"It's time," she said softly.

No words were needed between them. The world seemed to hold its breath around them. The soft rustling of leaves, the distant call of birds, and the gentle shift of light all felt like an accompaniment to the unspoken language they shared.

Mira didn't gesture for him to sit—he knew what to do. He sank down beside her, his legs crossed, a soft sigh escaping him as he settled into the quiet of the moment. There was no pressure to speak, no urgency to perform or seek. He was simply there, breathing, open, present.

Mira didn't break the silence, and neither did Noah. They sat there together, not needing words. After a long stretch of stillness, Mira reached into her bag, pulling out the journal Noah had once used. She handed it to him, its cover smooth, untouched by time.

Noah took it with reverence, the weight of it familiar in his hands. His fingers traced the pages, but they were blank.

His gaze lifted to Mira, seeking an explanation. But she only smiled, a soft, knowing smile.

"It always was," she said, her voice calm and without expectation.

Noah's heart stirred, and for the first time, he understood. The journal hadn't been a tool to be filled with answers—it had been a reflection, a mirror for him to see what was already there. Everything he needed was inside him.

He closed the journal, his fingers resting lightly on the cover. It wasn't empty—it was full of everything he had come to remember: peace, release, trust.

Mira didn't ask him to say anything. There was nothing left to say. The stillness between them was all that was needed. He smiled softly, the edges of his heart open, the question that had once driven him now gone.

The wind shifted gently over the water, and the quiet hum of nature filled the space between Noah and Mira. The sky was a soft blue, and the distant hills seemed to lean toward them, patient and still. The lake, as always, held its calm reflection.

Mira sat beside him, just as steady, her presence soft yet undeniably profound. She had never seemed like someone who needed to be understood in a conventional way. She was simply there—an echo in the quiet, an invitation to listen.

The silence stretched between them again, but this time, Noah felt something more. The stillness was not just external; it was internal, too. He felt the weight of his own breath, the pulse of life in his veins, the expansive sense of peace that had come to him over the course of his journey. It felt as if something was on the verge of unfolding, as though the moment itself was pregnant with meaning.

And then Mira spoke.

"I am not your guide," she said softly, her voice carrying the weight of a thousand untold truths. "I am your echo."

Noah's heart stilled for a moment. He turned toward her, his mind grasping for understanding.

She continued, her eyes meeting his with a steady, unblinking gaze. "I am not someone you met by chance. I am a reflection. A symbol. An embodiment of the voice within you—the one you silenced long ago."

The words didn't settle easily. They slipped through his mind, teasing the edges of something deeper. His thoughts swirled, trying to grasp the full meaning, but the logic, the explanation, eluded him. He had always thought of Mira as a teacher, someone guiding him to answers, someone who had unlocked the path for him. But now, there was a different sensation. It was as if the very ground beneath him was shifting, rearranging itself.

Mira's voice was soft but steady. "You wrote the journal, Noah. Long before you found it."

The words settled on his chest like a weight. He blinked, staring at her, but this time it wasn't the question he had held onto for so long that filled his mind—it was a sense of remembering. The journal. The blank pages. The deep, quiet work of his own hands. His own heart. The journey had been a rediscovery, an unraveling of something old that had never really been lost.

"You wrote the journal," she repeated, as if to anchor him to the truth of her words.

He felt it then, the familiar weight of the journal in his hands, not just as an object, but as a symbol of his own remembering. The voice he had been seeking was not outside him. It was the same voice that had been within him all along—silent, waiting to be heard. The Law of Release had never been something to find—it was something he had always known. Something he had lived.

Mira's smile was soft, knowing. "The journey you've been on was never about discovering something new. It was about letting go of what kept you from remembering."

The realization washed over Noah like a tide, gentle but undeniable. The line between what was external and what was internal blurred. Mira, the journal, the lessons—it wasn't something that had been outside of him. It was all a reflection, a mirror, a reminder of who he already was.

Noah sat in the quiet of the moment, his breath steady, his heart calm. It wasn't just that the world had changed—it was that he had. He had remembered. And that, he realized, was all that had ever been required.

Mira's presence beside him, soft as the breeze, was no longer a guide—it was a reflection of the path he had already walked. She had never been here to lead him. She had been here to remind him that he was already home.

The sunlight played in soft patterns on the water's surface, a gentle rhythm that matched the pace of Noah's breath. He sat in the stillness beside Mira, her presence a quiet anchor, as if the very air around them held secrets waiting to be remembered. The lake shimmered in the light, and Noah's mind began to stir with fragments, flashes of moments he had experienced with Mira—moments that, at the time, had felt ordinary but were now revealing themselves as something much deeper.

The train station, for instance. He remembered the way Mira had stood there, leaning against the pillar, as if waiting for something not yet spoken. She hadn't greeted him with answers or plans, just a look that seemed to say, *You're already here.* He had been so wrapped up in his confusion, in his need for answers, that he hadn't noticed the simplicity of her response.

Mira hadn't told him what to do. She hadn't led him. She had only asked questions.

"What does it feel like to stop running?" she had asked him on the platform. She hadn't said anything more. No advice. No instruction. She had simply left him with the question, the weight of it pressing softly on his chest. At the time, he had resisted the quiet, resisted the stillness that came with it. But now, as he sat beside her by the lake, he understood.

She wasn't here to fix him. She was here to make him see that he already had everything he needed. *What does it feel like to stop running?* She hadn't been asking for an answer. She had been inviting him to feel it, to realize it.

And the bookstore. He had thought he was seeking wisdom, that the bookshelves lined with titles were somehow the key. But Mira had simply said, *"What are you seeking when you seek the answers outside?"*

Her words hadn't been cryptic, but in that moment, they had felt like riddles. He had wanted to find the truth, to stumble upon something that would make everything clearer, but she had only pointed him inward. Her questions had always been invitations, not demands for a specific response. They were invitations to pause, to reflect.

Now, with the soft murmur of the lake behind them, Noah understood: *She never led. She reflected.*

All along, her questions had been like mirrors, designed to let him see himself more clearly. At the time, he had misunderstood them. He had looked for answers where there were none to be found. What Mira had been offering him was not a path to follow—it was a moment to pause, to turn inward, and to remember what was already there.

He remembered the walk they had taken in silence, the long stretch of forest where the only sound had been the crunch of leaves beneath their feet. There had been no need for words, and that, too, had been a part of the lesson. Mira's silence hadn't been absence; it had been presence. She had never needed to fill the space with anything. She had just been there, the steady, unwavering presence that he now recognized as something deeply familiar.

Her presence had always felt like home. Not the home of a place, but of a truth that he had known before, something deeper than time and space. It wasn't until now, as he sat with her again at the edge of the lake, that he could see it clearly. Mira had never been there to lead him on a journey of discovery. She had been there to help him remember the journey he had already walked, a journey that had led him back to himself.

As Noah looked at her now, sitting so calmly by the water, he felt the weight of everything shift. The pieces clicked into place. The journal had never been a guide—it had been a mirror. Mira had never been a teacher—she had been a reflection of his own knowing, his own remembering. He had written the journal long before he had found it, long before he had met her, because it was always inside of him.

Her riddles had never been puzzles to be solved—they had been invitations to uncover what was already there. And now, in this quiet moment by the lake, he understood the circle. The journey he had taken was not a path toward something new. It was a return to what had always been.

The circle was complete.

Noah's heart settled into a quiet understanding. Mira didn't need to speak again. The answers had never been hidden. They had been waiting for him all along, just beneath the surface. He smiled softly, the realization blooming inside him like the light filtering through the trees.

The lake, the journal, the questions, the silence—they weren't separate pieces. They were all part of the same whole, part of the same journey. And now, he was living it.

Mira's presence beside him was no longer a mystery. She was a part of him, the echo of his own voice, and he was ready to listen, to move forward, with everything he needed already within him.

Noah sat beside Mira, the calm lake stretching out before them, its surface smooth like glass. There was no urgency in the air, no push for understanding or insight. The moment was as it was—perfect in its simplicity. He could feel the subtle pull of the water's rhythm, its stillness mirroring the space inside him, a stillness that had grown over time, slowly but surely.

Mira looked at him, her gaze soft, full of knowing, but she said nothing. She simply nodded. Then, she asked him, almost gently, "Close your eyes, Noah."

He did. The world beyond his eyelids faded to nothing—the sounds of the water, the rustling leaves in the wind, even the subtle pulse of his own heartbeat—all of it softened, until there was only the silence.

Mira's presence remained. But it was not her voice that guided him now. It was the space between them, the air itself, as though the silence was speaking directly to him. It was not a place for words. Not a place for striving. It was a place for simply... being.

Noah breathed deeply, feeling the air move in and out of his body, slow and steady. His breath became the sound of the universe. It was the only thing that mattered in this moment. He was no longer a man seeking answers. He was the answer, just as the breath was the question and the response.

Mira's voice, soft and distant, echoed through his mind. "You already know. You always knew."

And it was in that quiet moment, in the space between her words, that something inside Noah released. It wasn't a dramatic shift. It wasn't a moment of revelation or grand understanding. It was a shift into something quieter, deeper—something that had always been there, waiting for him to recognize it.

He felt it first in his chest—an openness, a lightness. Then, it expanded outward, softening his mind, his shoulders, his entire being. There was nothing more to do. Nothing more to understand. Just the pure knowing that he was enough, as he was, right now.

Mira's presence, that unspoken connection, filled him. It was never about what she had taught him, never about the journal or the lessons. It was always about the space she held for him to find his own way back to himself. And in this moment, he realized—she had never left him. She had always been a reflection of what he was learning, what he was remembering, what he had always known deep inside.

He let the stillness settle into every cell of his being. In the silence, there was no more searching. No more striving. There was only trust—the kind of trust that comes from knowing the unseen is just as real as the seen.

And then, slowly, he opened his eyes.

Mira was gone. Not tragically. Not with a whisper of goodbye. She was simply... gone. There was no space for grief, no emptiness where she had been.

Because, in the stillness, Noah knew: she was never separate from him. She had never been anything other than an echo of the wisdom he already carried.

The lake shimmered in the light, the world around him unchanged. But Noah—he had changed. He no longer needed to seek or chase or prove. He understood now. The Law of Release wasn't a thing to grasp. It wasn't an answer to find. It was the act of trusting the space between the words, the silence that held everything together.

He stood slowly, feeling the fullness in his chest. There was no rushing, no waiting. Just the quiet, peaceful trust that everything was as it was meant to be. He was enough. He had always been enough.

And the moment stretched out, timeless and gentle, as Noah walked back to his life, no longer searching for something outside of himself, but living fully within the grace of all he had already found.

He smiled softly to himself, whispering, "Thank you."

And as the sunlight kissed the surface of the lake, Noah felt the pure, irreversible shift into inner trust.

Noah walked away from the lake, his feet treading softly on the familiar path that stretched before him. The earth felt different beneath his steps—grounded, yet alive, as though every stone and blade of grass was a reminder of how interconnected everything truly was. His pace was slower now, unhurried, with no destination in mind, just the simple act of being in motion.

He hummed a tune, a melody that seemed to come from somewhere deep inside, though he didn't recognize it. It felt like a song he had always known, but only now had the space to hear. The wind whispered through the trees, the birds calling to each other in the distance, and Noah felt the rhythm of it all. He wasn't in a hurry to reach the end of the path. There was no destination anymore. There was only this moment.

As he walked, he noticed the shift in how he saw the world. The sharpness, the tension that once dominated his perspective, had softened. He was no longer looking for something to fix or change; he was simply walking in harmony with everything around him.

Ahead, a woman stood on the path, her expression a mix of confusion and hesitation. She looked lost—perhaps physically, perhaps more deeply, in ways Noah couldn't fully see. But he did see her. And, in that moment, he knew exactly what she needed.

He slowed, the distance between them narrowing, and he smiled. Not out of pity or obligation, but out of a deep, genuine knowing. He met her gaze, and for the first time in a long time, the words that came to him felt simple, true, and filled with quiet peace.

"You're exactly where you're meant to be," he said.

The woman blinked, unsure. She smiled back, but there was a hesitation in her expression—an uncertainty that was real. Maybe she didn't fully understand the words, or maybe she did, but something in her paused, just for a moment. Something shifted.

Noah smiled softly, his heart light, and he continued on his way, the sound of his feet on the earth steady and calm. The woman lingered behind him, still standing there, her gaze distant.

He didn't look back. There was no need to. He had already given her what she needed—not in the form of advice, not in any grand gesture. Just a reminder—a soft reflection of the truth that lived in him, and now in her too.

As Noah walked on, he felt the weightlessness of it all, the sense that he was not alone, even in solitude. He wasn't Mira. He didn't carry the answers. But he had become something more—a quiet witness to the remembering that was happening in everyone, everywhere, all the time.

And in that knowing, he realized: We are all remembering.

The world stretched out before him, vast and full of possibility, but Noah no longer needed to seek it. The answers were already within him, in the stillness of the present, in the simplicity of each breath. The circle had completed itself, and a new one, just as quiet, just as gentle, had already begun.

PART 14: RECEPTIVITY – THE FINAL CHAPTER, THE FIRST STEP

A Letter Arrives—This Time, with an Invitation

The soft light of the morning sun filtered through the open window, casting gentle shadows across the kitchen table. Noah sat there, hands wrapped around a warm mug of tea, his gaze drifting out the window to the world beyond. The day was still young, and the air was cool—a perfect beginning. The steady hum of quiet was the only sound. It had become his favorite part of the day: the space between waking and doing, the brief moments where everything was just as it was, and he was simply present.

He sipped his tea, the warmth grounding him, his thoughts floating but not anchoring. He had no urgency, no desire to rush into anything. There was no "next step" hanging over him anymore—just this moment, here, in its fullness.

As he sat in that soft quiet, the sudden sound of something sliding under the door broke the stillness. At first, Noah didn't move—he wasn't expecting anything. But then, curiosity tugged at him, and he stood, walked to the door, and crouched down to retrieve the small envelope that had appeared.

The envelope was unassuming. No return address. No indication of its contents. But he could feel the weight of it in his hands, a quiet anticipation resting within the paper. He opened it, unfolded the note inside, and smiled when he read the familiar handwriting.

It was from Eden.

"We're starting a circle. A quiet one. Come sit with us."

There was no pressure, no urgency. Just the invitation, simple and unadorned. He felt the words settle in him, like a soft current beneath the surface of a still pond. A circle. A space for listening. For being present, without expectations.

Noah let the note rest in his hands for a moment longer. He didn't feel nervous, didn't feel uncertain. There was no need to prepare, no need to prove anything. The invitation wasn't about him taking on a role or becoming someone new—it was just about him showing up, as he was. He was no longer searching for answers; he was being asked to hold space. To be a witness.

He smiled again, the corners of his mouth softening. He could feel the shift in his own energy, as though, with this invitation, the final layers of his past had fallen away. He wasn't in a rush to solve the world, to fix what was broken. He was simply being asked to show up with what he had already become—someone who could hold the quiet. Someone who could be fully present, without needing to do anything.

The invitation was quiet, like the way the light stretched across his kitchen table, and it felt like it had been waiting for him all along.

Noah stood, walked to the window, and set the note on the sill, letting the morning sun catch the paper. He wasn't sure what the circle would look like or where it would lead. But he knew one thing: he was ready to be a part of it.

As he stood there, looking out at the world just beginning to stir, he felt that familiar peace settle in. The journey had never been about figuring everything out. It had always been about remembering—the gentle unfolding of truth, moment by moment. It wasn't a destination, but a way of being. And now, he was simply living it.

There was no grand finale waiting for him. The "next step" wasn't a revelation. It was a continuation—quiet, subtle, but full of possibility. It was the first step, over and over again, each time more deeply.

He was no longer seeking. He was receiving.

And for the first time in his life, that was enough.

The room was small but warm. Candles flickered softly, their flames stretching gently in the air, as though the room itself was breathing. Cushions were scattered across the floor, and soft light spilled through the windows, wrapping everything in a quiet embrace. A few people sat scattered around the room—some with their legs crossed, others reclining against the walls. There was no noise, no conversation, only the soft hum of people settling into their own stillness. It felt like the kind of space where something sacred could be found, even in the absence of words.

Noah walked into the room, his presence as unassuming as the space itself. He had been here once before—in this place, in this kind of circle—but this time, something was different. He wasn't the one seeking. He wasn't the one with questions. He was here to hold space, not to lead, not to impress. He had learned that there was no performance in true presence.

As he lowered himself onto one of the cushions, he felt the familiar warmth of the room settle around him. He wasn't here to fill the silence. He was here to share, gently. And as he sat, he realized: he didn't have answers, not really. But he had walked through fire, and he knew what it was to breathe in the smoke. That was what he could offer. He knew how to sit with the heat, how to remain steady when the world around you felt like it was burning.

Eden, who had invited him here, sat quietly across from him, her presence calm, open. She didn't speak. She simply looked at him with a softness that invited him to begin.

Noah took a slow breath, his chest rising and falling with the steady rhythm of the room. Then, in a voice that felt like it came from somewhere deep inside, he spoke. His words weren't polished or rehearsed. They were just truth, as simple and as raw as he could make them.

"I don't have advice," he began, his voice steady but soft. "I've never been one to offer solutions, but I've walked through fire, and I know how to breathe in the smoke."

There was no need for applause, no expectation of acknowledgment. He didn't need them to understand. But he noticed the shift in the room as soon as he spoke. One person, a woman sitting in the corner, began to quietly cry. Another person, a man with his eyes closed, nodded slowly, as if the weight of Noah's words had found a place inside him.

And that was it. That was the gift—the simplest thing, the most profound: the space to breathe, to feel, to sit with whatever was stirring inside them. There was no "fixing," no need to pull anyone from their pain. It was just presence. Pure and unadorned.

Noah sat quietly as the silence stretched out between them. He didn't need to speak again. He didn't need to fill the space with more words. Just his presence, just his simple act of sharing his story, had created something sacred in the room. He felt Mira in each of them—the soft reflection of truth, the quiet knowing that had always been there, waiting to be remembered. And, in that moment, he saw Mira in himself, too.

This was how it was meant to be. Not teaching. Not guiding. Just being.

The circle was a quiet, gentle holding of space. And Noah could see now that this was how healing happened. Not in grand gestures, not in grand speeches, but in the quiet act of witnessing, of simply being present with another's pain, another's joy.

And as the room settled back into its stillness, he realized: there was no more searching. This was the moment. This was the beginning of the rest of his life—not as a teacher, not as someone who had all the answers, but as someone who simply knew how to breathe. How to breathe with others. How to sit in the fire together.

And that, Noah knew, was enough.

The night air was crisp as Noah walked through the quiet streets. There was a stillness in the world, a gentle hum that seemed to carry the weight of the day's reflections. The stars were scattered across the sky like ancient, glowing secrets, and the moon hung low, its light casting long shadows on the ground.

He walked slowly, his footsteps quiet on the pavement, his thoughts light but profound. The circle had shifted something within him—a deepening, a knowing that wasn't bound by words or time. It was the simple truth of being, of holding space for himself and others. He felt it all now: the weight of the past, the peace of the present, and the openness of the future.

As he turned the corner, he came upon the bookstore—the same bookstore where he had first seen Mira. It was closed now, its windows dark, the lights inside turned off for the night. For a moment, Noah simply stood there, looking at the building. The memory of their first encounter lingered softly in his mind: the awkwardness, the curiosity, the unspoken recognition between them.

He smiled, the corners of his mouth lifting gently. A quiet gratitude filled his chest, and for a moment, he simply stood there—not longing, not seeking, just honoring the memory.

There was no ache. No yearning to go back to that moment, to recreate what had once been. He wasn't chasing after the past. He wasn't trying to find Mira again, to understand what had happened, or to relive their conversation. He had walked that path already. The answers were no longer out there—they were within him now, in the way he held space for himself, in the way he walked through life with awareness, with peace.

He bowed his head gently, a silent gesture of respect to the memory, to the lessons learned.

"Thank you," he whispered, his voice soft in the still night. "But I don't need to find you anymore."

And in that moment, there was nothing more to say. The words didn't need to be louder. The memory didn't need to be clung to. It had served its purpose. He had learned what he needed to learn. The past was not something to hold on to, but something to honor as part of his journey.

Noah took a slow breath, letting the air fill his lungs, and then he turned away from the bookstore, continuing his walk. He wasn't walking away from anything. He wasn't leaving something behind. He was simply living in the present moment, fully aware that everything he had experienced had led him to this place—not in time, but in awareness.

The journey was no longer about seeking. It was about being. It was about remembering, without holding on.

And as he walked, he felt the lightness of it—of the lesson, of the peace, of the knowing that he had everything he needed inside of him. He had no more need to search, to chase, to grasp. Everything was unfolding, just as it should.

And that was enough.

Noah arrived at the café early, as usual, before the rush of customers filled the small, cozy space. The scent of freshly brewed coffee mingled with the quiet murmur of soft jazz music playing in the background. He found a table by the window, the soft morning light spilling across the table.

It was a place he'd come to appreciate, not for its bustle, but for its stillness. A perfect space for receiving.

As he sat, he thought back to the circle the night before—the people he had sat with, the shared stories, the quiet moments of understanding. It had been a beautiful experience, and yet, he knew that something had shifted in him. Something deeper. The more he had allowed others to speak, the more he had allowed himself to listen—not just with his ears, but with his whole presence. And that was where the magic lay: in the space between words.

He didn't need to fix anyone. He didn't need to offer solutions. He simply needed to be present, to hold space for the unspoken. And that was enough.

The door to the café opened with a soft chime, and Noah looked up to see Ravi walk in. The young man's face was drawn, tired, and as he spotted Noah, he gave a small, hesitant wave. Ravi had been in the circle the night before. A quiet presence, someone who had carried a weight with him—something unspoken, a struggle Noah could sense but couldn't quite name.

Ravi approached the table and sat down, his shoulders slightly hunched as if he were carrying an invisible burden. He didn't speak immediately, just sat for a moment, looking down at his hands, folding and unfolding them nervously.

Noah smiled softly, but said nothing. He waited.

The quiet between them stretched out, comfortable yet charged. Ravi took a deep breath, his voice shaking as he finally spoke.

"I don't know where to start," he said, his eyes meeting Noah's. "I just—everything feels... so heavy. I don't know how to get out of it. I just keep going in circles, you know? I try to change things, but it's like nothing works. I'm lost." His voice broke as he spoke the last word, and Noah could see the tears that gathered at the corners of his eyes.

Noah remained silent, watching him with compassion, but offering no advice, no immediate comfort. He let the words hang in the air, felt the weight of them, and let Ravi feel the space to breathe.

Ravi let out a shaky breath, and then another. Slowly, the floodgates opened. He began speaking, not in a stream of conscious thought, but with a deep, raw honesty. Words spilled out about his family, his past, his mistakes, his fears. He spoke about his longing for peace, his need for approval, his constant battle to be seen, to be enough. The tears came freely now, but Noah didn't move. He didn't reach for tissues or try to comfort. He simply held space, letting the words flow without interference.

As Ravi spoke, he seemed to unravel before Noah. His shoulders relaxed a little. His voice grew softer, not from exhaustion, but from the release of so much that had been pent up. The weight he carried seemed to lessen with each word, and Noah could sense the quiet transformation happening, not because of any solution Noah had given, but because of the simple act of listening—letting someone be seen without judgment, without the need to fix.

When Ravi finally paused, his voice quiet, he wiped his eyes, looking at Noah, as if unsure of what to say next.

Noah sat still for a moment. Then, with a calmness that felt right, he spoke.

"No one's ever let me say all that without trying to fix me," Ravi said, his voice still fragile but relieved.

Noah smiled softly. "That's the Law of Release," he said, his voice low and steady. "Letting things be seen, not solved."

Ravi looked at him, his expression confused but open. "What do you mean?"

Noah leaned back slightly, his hands resting lightly on the table. "When we're struggling, when we're in pain, we often want answers. We want someone to tell us what to do, to fix things. But sometimes, what we really need is to be seen. To let everything come to the surface—without shame, without fear of judgment—and just... be. That's the release. It's not about solving the problem. It's about letting it exist, giving it space to breathe, to be felt."

Ravi's eyes softened as Noah spoke. He sat back in his chair, a gentle realization settling over him. The weight he had been carrying didn't disappear. But something had shifted. He wasn't alone in it anymore.

"No one's ever told me that," Ravi murmured, his voice quieter now, softer. "I always thought I had to fix myself, or make myself better somehow. But... maybe it's okay to just be where I am."

Noah nodded, his smile soft but sincere. "It's more than okay," he said. "It's the beginning of letting everything flow. You don't have to fix anything. You just have to let it be, let it move. And when you're ready, the next step will come."

For a moment, there was a quiet understanding between them. Ravi's breathing had steadied, his shoulders had loosened. The space between them had shifted, and Noah could feel the subtle change in the air. This was not about giving answers. It was about being present with someone's truth.

Ravi sat a little straighter now. "Thank you," he said, his voice quieter but full of something new—hope, perhaps, or maybe just a sense of relief.

Noah smiled gently, feeling the truth of the moment in his own heart. "You don't need to thank me. Just remember: you're exactly where you need to be."

And in that simple exchange, in the silence that followed, Noah felt it again—that deep knowing that the Law of Release was not about instruction or fixing, but about showing up as a mirror for others. It wasn't his role to solve anyone's pain. It was simply to witness it, to hold space for it to be seen, and in doing so, allow it to transform.

And just like that, he realized: the work wasn't in teaching. It was in listening.

Noah stood in the early morning light, the soft warmth of the sun brushing against his face as he stepped into the garden. The world around him seemed still, but full of promise. The earth was moist from a light rain the night before, and the air held that sweet, earthy scent that reminded him of all that was growing just beneath the surface—just waiting to be seen. He hadn't planned this moment, yet it felt perfect. As if he had been called to it, not by force, but by the quiet pull of something greater than himself.

He bent down and ran his fingers through the soil, feeling the coolness, the dampness, the life in the ground. He had come to this garden not to control it, but to nurture it, to witness it as it unfolded. He took a small sapling from a pot beside him—an oak tree, one that would take years to reach its full height—and gently placed it into the soil. As he did, he whispered to it, though he didn't know why. Maybe it was gratitude. Maybe it was a prayer.

"May you grow with ease," he murmured.

Noah stood for a moment longer, watching as the tree settled into its new home. His hands were muddy now, but there was something beautiful in that—the connection to earth, to growth, to the way life always found its own rhythm, even when it seemed slow or uncertain.

As he stood, he remembered the words he had written in his journal a few days before:

"Receptivity is not waiting. It's meeting life with an open hand."

He thought about the distinction. Receptivity wasn't about passively sitting back and waiting for things to happen. It wasn't surrendering to fate or letting life pass by without involvement. It was about meeting life head-on, but with an openness, an awareness, and a readiness to respond—not from a place of force, but from a place of trust.

As he continued to work in the garden, Noah reflected on how this understanding had begun to shape his life. He no longer approached things with a sense of urgency or striving. He didn't chase after outcomes or try to control the timing of events. Instead, he met each moment as it came, responding to it as it unfolded. He honored his boundaries and respected others'. He loved, not with the intensity of need, but with the gentle steadiness of someone who knew that love, like life itself, would bloom in its own time.

He moved from plant to plant, gently tending to them, not with a sense of duty, but with joy. This was the work of receptivity—not action for the sake of action, but intentional, mindful care. He was present, not waiting, not forcing things to grow. He simply nurtured what was already here.

Later that afternoon, after a slow walk through the woods, Noah returned to his journal. He felt drawn to write about his day, to capture this feeling of openness, of ease.

He wrote:

"Receptivity is not passive. It's not about waiting for something to happen. It's about being present to what is already here, knowing that everything comes to us in its time. Receptivity is trusting that the earth will nourish what we plant, even when we can't see its roots. It's giving space to things, letting them unfold in their own rhythm, even if it means waiting. It's knowing that the moment is always right, as it is, and that we are always enough. Receptivity is living with an open hand—not grabbing, not clutching, but offering and receiving."

Noah paused after he wrote those words, looking down at the page. There was no urgency in him now. No rushing. No striving for the next step. Just a quiet certainty that all was unfolding exactly as it should.

As he closed his journal, he glanced out the window at the tree he had planted earlier, now standing quietly in the garden. It was small, but it was strong, grounded in the earth, ready to grow at its own pace.

Noah smiled, a deep, quiet smile that reached his heart. He was no longer looking for something outside of himself. He was simply living, trusting, and responding to the world as it came, meeting each moment with an open hand.

Receptivity, he realized, was not a goal to be achieved. It was a way of being—a quiet, unforced dance with life, where everything was allowed to unfold in its own time. And he was content to simply be a part of that dance, knowing that he was always exactly where he needed to be.

Noah sat at his desk, the journal resting in front of him. He had held it so many times before, each page a testament to his journey. A journey that had unfolded not through striving, but through surrender, not through effort, but through trust. His hands, now steady and sure, gently opened the journal, revealing the still-blank pages.

He smiled, the smile of someone who no longer sought answers, but simply understood. The blankness didn't feel like emptiness. It felt like possibility.

There had been a time when he would have filled each page with questions—longings for something outside of himself, something to fix the broken parts of him. But now, he knew the truth: there was nothing to fix. There was only life to meet, to witness, to breathe with.

Noah picked up the pen, holding it lightly between his fingers. He stared at the blank page for a moment, the silence in the room filling him. This wasn't the end. He had known for a while now that there was no finality, no conclusion. There was only the continuous unfolding of the breath, the quiet rhythm of living.

He wrote, his handwriting flowing without hesitation:

"Release is not the end.

It's the breath between beginnings."

He paused, looking at the words for a moment, letting them settle into him. They weren't an answer. They were a truth, a truth he had lived. He set the pen down and closed the journal softly. Not in finality, but in recognition that it had served its purpose. The journal had never been a source of magic, but a mirror, a place to remember what he already knew.

And now, it was time to let it be. He no longer needed the pages to guide him. He had become the living expression of what he had written, what he had learned.

A soft knock at the door pulled him from his thoughts. He stood, his feet moving with quiet intention. As he opened the door, he found a young woman standing on the threshold, her eyes wide and unsure, her expression clouded with confusion—or perhaps, tears.

For a moment, she hesitated, as if unsure whether to step into the room, as if the weight of her emotions held her in place.

Noah smiled gently, the warmth of understanding in his eyes. He stepped aside, making space for her.

"Come in," he said, his voice soft but confident. "You're not late. You're right on time."

The woman looked at him, still unsure, but something in his presence began to settle the storm within her. She stepped inside, the door closing behind her with a quiet finality that felt, in that moment, like the beginning of something new.

Noah didn't know what her story was, but he knew she didn't need fixing. She didn't need answers. She needed space to breathe, to be seen, to remember.

As she sat down, Noah stood by the window for a moment, looking out at the world. The sun was setting, casting a soft light across the room, as if the world itself were breathing with him.

And then he turned back, his heart at peace. The circle, he realized, was not something that ever ended. It was an ongoing dance, one of being, of receptivity, of presence.

And this moment—the one where he held space for someone else—was the next step, the next breath, in an endless flow of unfolding.

Noah smiled quietly to himself, not out of pride, but out of understanding. The journey was never finished. It was simply lived. And the circle, like life itself, would continue.

As the woman settled in, Noah felt the fullness of the moment. Not the fullness of answers, but the fullness of connection. Of shared humanity. Of quiet, eternal truth.

And so, he sat down, not as a teacher, but as a mirror. Not as someone with all the answers, but as someone who knew the power of silence, the power of simply being present. The circle had begun again. And this, he knew, was exactly how it was meant to be.

END.

Epilogue
The Echo of Stillness

There are stories we tell to find ourselves.

And then there are stories that help us remember we were never lost.

Noah's path wasn't linear. It was a spiral—each return a deepening, each step forward a soft letting go. The Law of Release did not lead him to a perfect life. It led him to a present one.

There were still moments of sadness. Still echoes of old fears. But they no longer ruled him. He met them the way the earth meets rain: without resistance. Open. Absorbing. Alive.

Sometimes, he would sit by the lake—alone, or with someone new beside him. Not to teach, but to witness. Sometimes, he would walk the city streets, pausing for a moment of stillness between the noise. And sometimes, he would say nothing at all, trusting that presence spoke louder than words ever could.

He never became a guru. Never published a book of lessons. But somehow, his way of being became an offering. An unspoken invitation:

You don't have to force.
You don't have to grip.
You can live with an open hand.

People came and went. Some stayed. Some returned. And all, in their own way, remembered something soft and sacred in his presence.

The journal remained closed on his shelf—not as a relic, but as a reminder. He no longer needed to write the truth.

He *was* the truth, lived.

In the quiet hours of the morning, he would still make tea. Still watch the light shift on the walls. Still smile at nothing in particular.

Because peace was no longer a destination.

It was his home.

And somewhere, a new knock would come. A new soul searching for air.

And Noah, with his quiet smile, would open the door—not with answers, but with space.

Because the circle continues.

Because remembering is never finished.

Because in every breath,

we begin again.

—*Vincent WB, The Law of Release*

Appendix: Gentle Practices for Everyday Release

This book was never about giving steps—but if you're wondering how to begin applying the Law of Release in your life, here are a few quiet invitations. These are not tasks. They're doorways.

1. The One-Breath Pause

When you feel overwhelmed, stop for just one breath. Feel it enter. Feel it leave. That's all. That's the reset.

2. The Open-Hand Journal Prompt

Each morning or evening, ask:
What am I holding too tightly?
What wants to be released today?

3. Sit Without Solving

Once a day, sit for 5 minutes. Don't fix. Don't analyze. Just be. Let what rises... rise. Let what passes... pass.

4. The Gentle Goodbye

When releasing something—a thought, a fear, even a person—don't force it. Say softly:
"Thank you for what you were. I set you free."

5. The Mirror Moment

Stand in front of the mirror. Look into your own eyes and say:
"You are already enough. Even now."

These aren't habits to master.

They're invitations to remember.

Index

GIFT NOTE

A Gift for You

Dear ....

This book is more than just pages and words—it is a gift of possibility, a journey of transformation, and an invitation to live with grace, peace, and openness. May you find within these pages the courage to release what no longer serves you, the wisdom to embrace the present, and the joy of being fully yourself in every moment.

If you've received this book as a gift, know that it was chosen with care, knowing that your path is one of growth, discovery, and remembering. May it inspire you to trust in the process of life, to let go of fear, and to open your heart to all that is waiting for you.

With love and light,

....

(PS: Keep breathing—everything you need is already within you.)

Did you love *The Law Of Release: Moving From Resistance To Receptivity*? Then you should read *The Law Of Detachment*[1] by VINCENT WB and FAITH JK!

[2]

The Law of Detachment: Embrace Freedom Through Letting Go" is a powerful guide to understanding the transformative practice of detachment. In this book, you'll discover how releasing control, attachments, and expectations can unlock a deeper sense of peace, clarity, and freedom in your life. Through heartfelt storytelling, practical wisdom, and real-life examples, **"The Law of Detachment"** shows you that true growth happens when we learn to let go—not of our dreams or desires, but of the fear and emotional baggage that weigh us down.

---

1. https://books2read.com/u/4jO7KY

2. https://books2read.com/u/4jO7KY

If you've ever felt stuck, overwhelmed, or burdened by the need for control, this book will help you break free. Learn how to embrace the flow of life, trust the journey, and find strength in surrender. **"The Law of Detachment"** is more than just a philosophy; it's a way of living that will empower you to find peace, joy, and resilience in every moment.

Are you ready to let go and unlock the power of your truest self? This book is your key to a life of limitless possibility and effortless peace.

Also by VINCENT WB

Shadows on Sapphire Hill
The Silent Whispers
The Web of Lies
The Shattered Truth
The Reckoning at Sapphire Hill
The Last Echo

The Silent Witness Files
The Unspoken Truth
Shadows of the Mind
The Silent Syndicate
The Revenant's Last Secret

Standalone
Infinite Romance; Love's Soft Melody
The Law Of Detachment
The Universal Code, 369 Rule
The Lighthouse Keeper's Secret, A Tale of Trust and Transformation
How to Bake the Perfect Chocolate Cake, A Decadent Guide for
Dessert Lovers

Elara and the Astral Library
After the Rain
The Playlist of Our Lives
Designing Your Dream Life; A Step by Step Guide
The Resilience Roadmap; A Journey of Falling, Rising, and Becoming Unstoppable
The Law of Reality: A Novel of Perception, Power, and Transformation.
The Eagle's View: Thinking Beyond Limits and Soaring High
The 5am Myth: Why Early Risers Don't Always Win
Breaking the Cycle: Escape Mediocrity and Rewrite Your Story
The Sunbeam Strategy: Small Steps That Lead to Massive Success
Scorch The Doubt: The Mental Shift To Unshakable Confidence
The Law Of Release: Moving From Resistance To Receptivity

Printed by Libri Plureos GmbH in Hamburg,
Germany